POLITICAL SUICIDE

POLITICAL SUICIDE

THE FIGHT FOR THE SOUL
OF THE DEMOCRATIC PARTY

TED RALL

NEW YORK / OAKLAND / LIVERPOOL

ACKNOWLEDGMENTS

Thanks to James Taranto of the *Wall Street Journal*, who gave me the space to explore the subject of this book in his pages.

Also to Dan Simon, who not only published this book but provided his superb editing skills. Lauren Hooker as always was an excellent copy editor.

As always thank you to my agent Sandy Dijkstra and her compadre Elise Capron. Thanks most of all to the Democratic National Committee for its ongoing reliable corruption.

■   ■   ■

A Seven Stories Press First Edition

Seven Stories Press
140 Watts Street
New York, NY 10013
www.sevenstories.com

Library of Congress Cataloging-in-Publication Data

Names: Rall, Ted, author.
Title: Political suicide : the fight for the soul of the Democratic party /
    Ted Rall.
Description: First edition. | New York : Seven Stories Press, [2020]
Identifiers: LCCN 2020014788 (print) | LCCN 2020014789 (ebook) | ISBN
    9781609809942 (trade paperback) | ISBN 9781609809959 (ebook)
Subjects: LCSH: Democratic Party (U.S.) | Progressivism (United States
    politics) | United States--Politics and government--21st century.
Classification: LCC JK2316 .R35 2020 (print) | LCC JK2316 (ebook) | DDC
    324.2736--dc23
LC record available at https://lccn.loc.gov/2020014788
LC ebook record available at https://lccn.loc.gov/2020014789

Printed in the USA.

9 8 7 6 5 4 3 2 1

POLITICAL
SUICIDE

WHEN BERNIE
MET HILLARY

JUNE 2016:

HILLARY CLINTON IS PREPARING
TO DECLARE VICTORY
OVER BERNIE SANDERS.

WIKILEAKS CHOOSES THIS MOMENT TO RELEASE NEARLY 20,000 EMAILS SENT BY TOP OFFICIALS OF THE DEMOCRATIC NATIONAL COMMITTEE FROM JANUARY 2015 THROUGH MAY 2016, THE PERIOD OF SANDERS'S STUNNING RISE.

Wikileaks releases thousands of emails involving DNC & Clinton campaign

DNC Email Archive

This releases contains 19,252 emails and 8,034 attachments from the top of the US Democratic National Committee (DNC) and is part of our Hillary Leaks series. The leaks come from the accounts of seven key figures in (...)

Posted: Fri 10:05 PM, Jul 22, 2016

Leaked DNC emails reveal details of anti-Sanders sentiment

Days before convention, cache of 19,000 emails released and several show officials scoffing at Hillary Clinton's former rival and questioning his religion

The 4 Most Damaging Emails From the DNC WikiLeaks Dump

WikiLeaks leaked nearly 20,000 emails on Friday from top DNC officials.

By ALANA ABRAMSON and SHUSHANNAH WALSHE
July 25, 2016, 11:13 AM · 5 min read

ACCORDING TO ITS OWN RULES, THE DNC IS SUPPOSED TO BE NEUTRAL. HOWEVER, THE LEAKED EMAILS SHOWED A DISGUSTING BIAS IN FAVOR OF HILLARY CLINTON.

THE ANIMUS IS CLEAR:

Democratic National Committee CFO Brad Marshall,
May 5, 2016 :

From:MARSHALL@dnc.org
To: MirandaL@dnc.org, PaustenbachM@dnc.org, DaceyA@dnc.org
Date: 2016-05-05 03:31
Subject: No shit

It might may no difference, but for KY and WVA can we get someone to ask his belief. Does he believe in a God. He had skated on saying he has a Jewish heritage. I think I read he is an atheist. This could make several points difference with my peeps. My Southern Baptist peeps would draw a big difference between a Jew and an atheist.

DNC Chairman Debbie Wasserman Schultz,
describing Sanders campaign manager
Jeff Weaver,
May 13, 2016 :

From:hrtsleeve@gmail.com
To: PaustenbachM@dnc.org
Date: 2016-05-13 17:21
Subject: Re: Weaver: "I think we should go to the convention"

He is an ASS.

DWS

DNC National Secretary Mark Paustenbach to National Communications Director Luis Miranda, May 21, 2016:

```
From:markpaustenbach@gmail.com
To: mirandal@dnc.org
Date: 2016-05-21 22:23
Subject: Bernie narrative
```

Wondering if there's a good Bernie narrative for a story, which is that Bernie never ever had his act together, that his campaign was a mess.

Specifically, DWS had to call Bernie directly in order to get the campaign to do things because they'd either ignored or forgotten to something critical.

She had to call Bernie after the data breach to make his staff to respond to our concerns. Even then they didn't get back to us, which is why we had to shut off their access in order to get them to finally let us know exactly how they snooped around HFA's data.

Same was true with the standing committee appointments. They never got back to us with their names (HFA and even O'Malley got there's in six weeks earlier) for the committees. So, again, the chair had to call Bernie personally for his staff to finally get us critical information. So, they gave us an awful list just a few days before we had to make the announcements.

It's not a DNC conspiracy, it's because they never had their act together.

THE EMAILS CONFIRM WHAT SANDERS'S CAMPAIGN HAS KNOWN FROM THE START: THE DEMOCRATIC PARTY LEADERSHIP IS DETERMINED TO RIG THE 2016 PRIMARIES AGAINST SANDERS.

THROUGHOUT THE 2016 DEMOCRATIC
PRIMARIES TRACKING POLLS SHOW THAT
SANDERS WOULD HANDILY DEFEAT TRUMP IN
A HEAD-TO-HEAD MATCHUP, WHEREAS
CLINTON WOULD HAVE MORE DIFFICULTY.

Poll: Bernie Sanders would beat Donald Trump

By Chris Moody, CNN Senior Digital Correspondent
Updated 3:11 PM ET, Thu July 30, 2015

Polls: Sanders has more potential to beat Trump

Recent data show Sanders has double-digit lead in support over Republican candidate while Clinton would face tight race.

by **Ryan Rifai**   f y
14 May 2016

When respondents in our NBC News/SurveyMonkey Weekly Election Tracking Poll were asked whether they would cast a vote for Trump or either of the Democratic candidates still in the race, Sanders is the favorite over Trump by 13 points.

Clinton also beats Trump, but the race is decidedly closer – 49 percent to 44 percent. These results are according to the latest from

DONALD TRUMP BECOMES PRESIDENT
BECAUSE THE DNC HAS ITS THUMB ON THE
SCALE FOR HILLARY.

IN APRIL 2015, WHEN SANDERS, AN
INDEPENDENT AND SELF-DESCRIBED
DEMOCRATIC SOCIALIST, ANNOUNCES HIS
RUN FOR PRESIDENT, CLINTON HAS LITTLE
REASON TO BE WORRIED.

BERNIE IS POLLING AT 4%.

Bernie Sanders, Long-Serving Independent, Enters Presidential Race as a Democrat

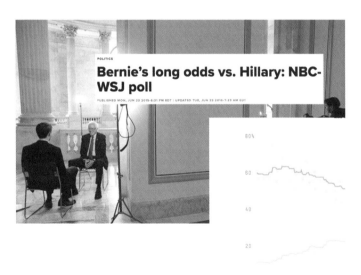

POLITICS

Bernie's long odds vs. Hillary: NBC-WSJ poll

PUBLISHED MON, JUN 22 2015-6:31 PM EDT | UPDATED TUE, JUN 23 2015-7:29 AM EDT

BUT SANDERS'S CAMPAIGN QUICKLY GATHERS MOMENTUM. HIS SUPPORTERS, ENERGIZED BY THE FIRST UNABASHEDLY LEFTIST CANDIDATE FOR PRESIDENT IN MEMORY, FILL 10,000-SEAT STADIUMS.

WITHIN A YEAR, THE SOCIALIST FROM VERMONT HAS PULLED VIRTUALLY NECK-AND-NECK WITH CLINTON: 43% TO 46%, WITHIN THE MARGIN OF ERROR.

CLINTON IS WELL KNOWN. SANDERS IS RELATIVELY OBSCURE. THAT BENEFITS CLINTON. SO THE DNC PULLS ONE OF THEIR TYPICAL DIRTY TRICKS. TO DEPRIVE SANDERS OF EXPOSURE, THE CLINTON-CONTROLLED DNC SCHEDULES ITS DEBATES ON WEEKEND NIGHTS WHEN TV VIEWERSHIP IS LOW.

"But when Democratic debates are scheduled during sports playoffs and holiday shopping seasons, you have to wonder whether the DNC actually wants anyone to see them."

—Haley Morris, spokesperson for former Maryland governor Martin O'Malley

ANOTHER NASTY TURN INVOLVES "SUPERDELEGATES"—PARTY INSIDERS GIVEN DELEGATE SEATS AND NOMINATING VOTES.

SUPERDELEGATES ARE SUPPOSED TO KEEP THEIR PREFERENCES TO THEMSELVES. PROMPTED BY THE DNC, HOWEVER, NEARLY ALL ANNOUNCE THEIR LOPSIDED SUPPORT FOR CLINTON. NO MATTER HOW MANY PRIMARIES AND CAUCUSES SANDERS WINS, DELEGATE COUNTS ON TV NEWS SIGNAL THAT HE WILL NEVER CATCH UP TO HILLARY.

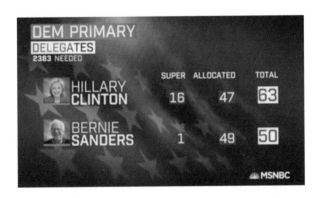

"Sanders went to bed ahead [in New Hampshire] and he woke up effectively tied [in the delegate count]."

—Christine Pelosi, a DNC member from California

THE DNC IS MILLIONS OF DOLLARS IN DEBT.
CLINTON SEES HER CHANCE.

SHE AGREES TO RAISE ENOUGH MONEY IN A
"HILLARY VICTORY FUND" TO FUND THE
PARTY'S DATA, TECH, ANALYTICS,
RESEARCH, AND COMMUNICATIONS—IN
EXCHANGE FOR CONTROL. THE DNC GIVES
CLINTON THE RIGHT TO CHOOSE THE
PARTY'S PERSONNEL. THERE IS NO EVIDENCE
THAT THEY OFFER A SIMILAR DEAL TO
BERNIE.

"This was not a criminal act, but as I saw it, it
compromised the party's integrity."
—Donna Brazile

When Bernie Met Hillary...

BETWEEN WIKILEAKS AND BRAZILE (WHO WILL BECOME DNC CHAIRMAN AFTER WASSERMAN SCHULTZ IS FORCED TO RESIGN), THE DNC CORRUPTION IS IMPOSSIBLE TO DENY (THOUGH THEY TRY!).

BUT 2016 IS NO OUTLIER. THERE IS A GROUNDHOG DAY-LIKE REPEATING OF HISTORY: PROGRESSIVE CANDIDATES FIGHTING FOR THE ISSUES THAT MATTER TO PEOPLE AND THE DEMOCRATIC ESTABLISHMENT UNDERMINING THE ISSUES AND THE CANDIDATES.

HILLARY CLINTON AND HER HUSBAND MADE $130 MILLION GIVING SPEECHES TO WALL ST. AND HAD $42 MILLION IN HER CAMPAIGN WAR CHEST.

DONALD TRUMP HAD JUST $1 MILLION. AND HE REFUSED TO SHOW HIS TAXES BECAUSE HE'S NOT REALLY THAT RICH.

SHE PRETENDED TO BE A WOMAN OF THE PEOPLE.

HE PRETENDED TO BE WORTH $10 BILLION.

WANNA SWITCH?

PROGRESSIVES KNOW THEY'VE BEEN CHEATED. ENOUGH BERNIE-OR-BUSTERS STAY HOME IN NOVEMBER 2016, OR CAST PROTEST VOTES FOR TRUMP, TO DENY HILLARY CLINTON THE PRESIDENCY.

THOUGH TRUMP LOSES THE POPULAR VOTE, HE WINS THE GENERAL ELECTION.

NEWLY ELECTED PRESIDENT DONALD TRUMP
GOVERNS LIKE PREVIOUS ILLEGITIMATELY
ELECTED REPUBLICANS SUCH AS GEORGE W.
BUSH.

WITHOUT ANY PRETENSE OF COMPROMISE,
HE ISSUES A FLURRY OF EXECUTIVE ORDERS
TO ENACT HARD-RIGHT POLICIES: A BAN ON
MUSLIMS VISITING THE U.S., THE FORCIBLE
SEPARATION OF MIGRANT CHILDREN FROM
THEIR PARENTS AT THE U.S.-MEXICO BORDER.

HE PUSHES A HUGE TAX CUT FOR WEALTHY
INDIVIDUALS AND BIG CORPORATIONS VIA A
PARTY-LINE VOTE.

OTHER COUNTRIES USED TO LOOK UP TO US. THAT WAS AN IMPORTANT PART OF WHAT WE AMERICANS THOUGHT MADE US AN IMPORTANT COUNTRY.

NOT ANYMORE.

THANKS TO THIS ARROGANT, WILLFULLY IGNORANT BLOWHARD, THE UNITED STATES BECOMES AN INTERNATIONAL PARIAH AND LAUGHINGSTOCK.

THE CENTRISTS WHO HAVE DOMINATED DEMOCRATIC PARTY POLITICS SINCE THE 1970s ARE DISCREDITED. PROGRESSIVES, LONG OUT IN THE COLD AND TAKEN FOR GRANTED, FINALLY HAVE THEIR CHANCE.

THE CRISIS THAT THE ESTABLISHMENT AND
RECENT DEMOCRATIC AND REPUBLICAN
REGIMES HAVE GOT US INTO HAS CREATED
AN OPPORTUNITY LIKE NEVER BEFORE TO
REMAKE THE DEMOCRATIC PARTY AS A
TRULY PROGRESSIVE ORGANIZATION, ONE
THAT ACTUALLY SERVES THE PEOPLE.

BUT THE ENTRENCHED, STATE-LIKE
APPARATUS THAT IS THE DEMOCRATIC
PARTY MACHINE STILL BELONGS TO THE
CLINTONS AND THEIR CHUMS.

BECAUSE THESE THIRD WAY/DEMOCRATIC LEADERSHIP COUNCIL/CENTRIST "MODERATES" FEAR LOSING CONTROL OF THE DEMOCRATIC PARTY, THEY HATE THEIR PARTY'S OWN PROGRESSIVE WING (WHICH COMPRISES SEVEN OUT OF TEN VOTERS, A SIZABLE MAJORITY) MORE THAN THEY HATE THE REPUBLICAN RIGHT WING.

THE SIREN SONG OF THE MODERATE

THEY WOULD RATHER LOSE TO RACIST RIGHT-WING REPUBLICANS THAN WIN AS PROGRESSIVE DEMOCRATS!

THE SURPRISE VICTORY OF THE
CONGRESSWOMAN FROM QUEENS,
DEMOCRATIC SOCIALIST AND BERNIE
SUPPORTER ALEXANDRIA OCASIO-CORTEZ,
OVER CENTRIST DEMOCRATIC PARTY POWER-
HOUSE JOE CROWLEY IS A WAKE-UP CALL
TO ENTRENCHED POWERS WITHIN THE DNC.
BUT NOT THE KIND OF WAKE-UP CALL YOU
MIGHT BE IMAGINING.

HER WIN GIVES US A BONA FIDE SUPERNOVA
WHO CAN REPRESENT A NEW GENERATION OF
VOTERS AND LEAD US TOWARD WINNING THE
BATTLE FOR THE FUTURE OF AMERICA. BUT
THE DNC DRAWS THE EXACT OPPOSITE
LESSON: FIGHT HARDER THAN EVER AGAINST
THE NEW PROGRESSIVE WING.

GIVE UP THEIR POWER FOR THE GREATER
GOOD? NEVER.

THE POWER STRUGGLE BETWEEN THE PROGRESSIVE AND ESTABLISHMENT WINGS OF THE DEMOCRATIC PARTY CONTINUES TODAY. IN MANY WAYS, IT HAS GOTTEN WORSE.

FRAME GAME
Centrists vs. Progressives

Centrists vs. Progressives

By WILLIAM SALETAN   AUG 22, 1997

DEMOCRATS | AUG. 10, 2018

What Is a 'Centrist' Democrat, Anyway?

DEMOCRATS   GOVERNMENT   ELECTION DEBATES

Centrist Democrats Want You to Think They're the Big Boys on the Stage

To stall the progressive momentum, the centrists are trying to recast their ideas as more pragmatic. The problem is, they're not.

By Elie Mystal ✈

OCTOBER 17, 2019

Published on Friday, October 25, 2019 by Common Dreams

Centrists—Or Neoliberals–Control the Party and the Media and They're Risking Losing to Trump Again in 2020

We either ignite a revolution built around values, and take back the country from the neoliberal centrists, or we risk another Trump victory.
by John Atcheson

30

THIS TIME AROUND, AS WE CONTEMPLATE THE NEXT FOUR YEARS, THE STAKES HAVE GOTTEN EVEN HIGHER.

WHICH TRUMP **WILL WE GET**?

AS WE'VE SEEN WITH PREVIOUS BAD PRESIDENTS, LAWS AND POLICIES ARE EASIER TO ENACT THAN TO REPEAL. TRUMPISM WILL BE WITH US FOR YEARS.

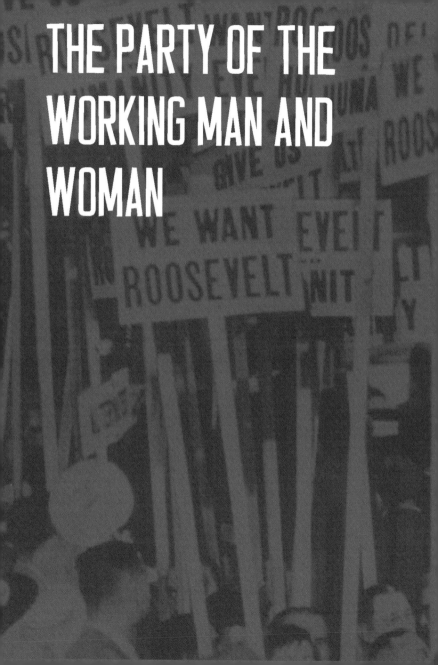

THE PARTY OF THE WORKING MAN AND WOMAN

THE MYTHOLOGY THAT DEMOCRATS
DEFEND WORKING MEN AND WOMEN
AGAINST MONIED INTERESTS
ORIGINATES IN THE GREAT POLITICAL
REALIGNMENT OF 1932 AND THE
ELECTION OF FDR, WHEN BLACKS
SWITCHED THEIR VOTES AWAY FROM
THE PARTY OF LINCOLN TO THE
DEMOCRATS.

NEW DEAL DEMOCRATS GROUNDED
THEIR WORLDVIEW IN FDR'S
TRIUMPH OVER THE GREAT
DEPRESSION.

ROOSEVELT BEAT BACK MASS
UNEMPLOYMENT WITH KEYNESIAN
GOVERNMENT SPENDING ON NEW
PROGRAMS, INCLUDING THE DIRECT
HIRING OF MILLIONS OF WORKERS.

Our Job with the WPA - Workers Handbook   Harry L. Hopkins Administrator

ROOSEVELT REINED IN BIG BUSINESS WITH NEW REGULATIONS. HE PROMOTED LABOR UNIONS.

"We had to struggle with the old enemies of peace—business and financial monopoly, speculation, reckless banking, class antagonism, sectionalism, war profiteering...

Never before in all our history have these forces been so united against one candidate as they stand today. They are unanimous in their hate for me—and I welcome their hatred."

—FDR, 1936

FDR'S PHILOSOPHY FORMED
THE BASIS OF DEMOCRATIC
PARTY THINKING FOR A HALF-
CENTURY:

GOVERNMENT SHOULD SPEND
MONEY TO HELP THE AVERAGE
JOE AND JANE. CAPITALISM
MUST BE STRICTLY REGULATED.

NEW DEAL DEMOCRATS WERE STRONG
ON ECONOMIC JUSTICE. ON OTHER
FORMS OF JUSTICE, NOT SO MUCH.

MORE SECURITY FOR
THE AMERICAN FAMILY

THE WIDOW OF A QUALIFIED
WORKER WILL RECEIVE MONTHLY
BENEFITS AT AGE 65. IN CERTAIN
CASES, AN AGED DEPENDENT
PARENT MAY GET BENEFITS. ...

FOR INFORMATION WRITE OR CALL AT THE NEAREST FIELD OFFICE OF THE
SOCIAL SECURITY BOARD

THOUGH DEMOCRATS DISAPPROVED OF RACISM, SEXISM, AND DISCRIMINATION GENERALLY, THESE STRUGGLES TOOK A BACK SEAT TO THE PRIORITY OF IMPROVING WAGES AND BENEFITS FOR THE AVERAGE (WHITE) AMERICAN, WHO WAS ASSUMED TO WORK IN A FACTORY.

THE WHITE WORKING CLASS OF THE MID-20TH CENTURY WAS HARDLY HOMOGENOUS.

WORKERS WERE DIVIDED BY NATION OF ORIGIN (GERMAN, ITALIAN, EASTERN EUROPEAN, ENGLISH, IRISH, ETC.), RELIGION (PROTESTANT AND CATHOLIC), AND REGION (NORTH AGAINST SOUTH).

AFRICAN AMERICANS AND JEWS WERE IMPORTANT TO THE NEW DEAL DEMOCRATIC COALITION. BUT AT THE TIME, JEWS, ITALIANS, AND THE IRISH WERE NOT CONSIDERED TO BE AS WHITE AS WHITE FOLK OF ENGLISH OR GERMAN DESCENT.

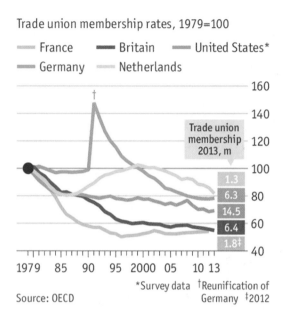

Trade union membership rates, 1979=100

━━ France ━━ Britain ━━ United States*
━━ Germany ━━ Netherlands

Trade union membership 2013, m

1.3
6.3
14.5
6.4
1.8‡

† Reunification of Germany

1979 85 90 95 2000 05 10 13

*Survey data † Reunification of
Germany ‡2012

Source: OECD

AFTER FDR DIED, DEINDUSTRIALIZATION
AND A POSTWAR BOOM PROPELLED
WORKERS' ASCENSION INTO THE MIDDLE
CLASS. THIS WAS GOOD NEWS, BUT IT
REDUCED THE RANKS OF THE UNIONS
THAT FORMED THE DEMOCRATIC BASE.

NEXT CAME THE CIVIL RIGHTS MOVEMENT OF THE 1960s.

THE STRUGGLE FOR RACIAL EQUALITY BROUGHT SOME GROUPS TOGETHER, ESPECIALLY AFRICAN AMERICAN AND JEWISH ACTIVISTS. BUT IT ALSO DROVE A WEDGE BETWEEN AFRICAN AMERICANS AND ETHNIC WHITES. REPUBLICANS SUCH AS RICHARD NIXON EXPLOITED THIS RIFT IN THE DEMOCRATIC COALITION.

FEMINISM, GAY RIGHTS, AND OTHER
IDENTITY MOVEMENTS DEEPENED THE
CULTURAL DIVIDE BETWEEN LIBERALS
AND WORKERS.

THROUGHOUT THE 1940s, 1950s, AND 1960s, DEMOCRATS SOLDIERED ON.

THEY REMADE THE ECONOMIC AND SOCIAL COMPACT WITH AMERICAN WORKERS BY PROTECTING FDR'S NEW DEAL AND EXPANDING IT INTO HARRY TRUMAN'S FAIR DEAL AND LBJ'S GREAT SOCIETY SLATE OF PROGRAMS.

TUCSON, ARIZONA, SATURDAY MORNING, JULY 31, 1965   MA 2-5855   TWENTY-SIX PAGES

Chapter In Medical History Begins

With Ex-President Truman Looking On

Medicare Is Signed Into Law By LBJ

One Of Eight In U.S.

Arizona Guard Gets Priority Tag

Plan Fulfills U.S. Dream, Says President

$6.5 Billion Program Hailed By Johnson, As 'Giving Hope To Older Americans'

Union Threatens ike On Sept. 1

Reds Renew Offensive In Viet Nam

Clouds Strike Picture

Teamsters Veto New Master Labor Pact

U.S. Steps Up

New Cabinet Post Is In The Making

ALL THE WHILE, FRACTURES IN THE COALITION BECAME INCREASINGLY VISIBLE.

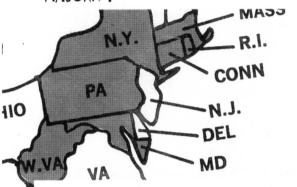

AS KEVIN PHILLIPS WROTE IN HIS 1969 BOOK *THE EMERGING REPUBLICAN MAJORITY*:

"Opposition to the welfare liberalism of the federal government...came in large part from prospering Democrats who objected to Washington dissipating their tax dollars on programs which did them no good. The Democratic Party fell victim to the ideological impetus of a liberalism which had carried it beyond programs taxing the few for the benefit of the many...to programs taxing the many on behalf of the few."

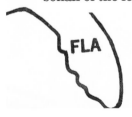

☐ Nixon
▨ Humphrey
⦂ Wallace

46

NIXON'S "SOUTHERN STRATEGY" LURED RACIST WHITES AWAY FROM THE DEMOCRATS. HIS PLEA TO A "SILENT MAJORITY" CONVINCED SOME VOTERS ANNOYED BY THE COUNTERCULTURE TO VOTE REPUBLICAN.

THE DEMOCRATIC PARTY FOUND ITSELF IN A CRISIS, ONE THAT PREVENTED IT FROM CAPITALIZING ON THE VACUUM CREATED BY THE COLLAPSE OF NIXONISM.

EVEN IN THE IMMEDIATE AFTERMATH OF THE WATERGATE BREAK-IN, GEORGE McGOVERN LOST THE 1972 PRESIDENTIAL ELECTION TO NIXON, WHO WAS REELECTED IN A LANDSLIDE.

EERILY PRESAGING THE CURRENT SPLIT,
THE PROGRESSIVE AND CORPORATE/
CENTRIST WINGS OF THE PARTY BLAMED
EACH ANOTHER FOR THE 1972 DISASTER.

EACH FACTION ARGUED THAT THE OTHER
HAD FORFEITED THE RIGHT TO DETERMINE
THE PARTY'S FUTURE DIRECTION AND
THAT IT ALONE ENJOYED LEGITIMACY.

WATERGATE BROUGHT DOWN PRESIDENT
NIXON AND PROMPTED A DEMOCRATIC
SWEEP IN THE 1974 MIDTERM ELECTIONS.

GIVEN THE DEVASTATING SCALE OF THE
IMPEACHMENT SCANDAL, ONE MIGHT HAVE
BEEN FORGIVEN FOR ASSUMING THERE
WOULD BE A PROLONGED PERIOD OF
DEMOCRATIC DOMINANCE TO FOLLOW.

THOUGH THEY HAD COME TOGETHER FOR
RADICAL SOCIAL CHANGE AND TO END THE
VIETNAM WAR, THE AMERICAN LEFT FOUND
ITSELF EXHAUSTED, DEMORALIZED, AND IN
NO CONDITION TO FEND OFF A CABAL OF
CONSERVATIVE DEMOCRATS WHO WOULD
GO ON TO RULE THE PARTY: FIGURES LIKE
"SCOOP" JACKSON, RICHARD GEPHARDT, AL
GORE, BILL BRADLEY, AND JOE LIEBERMAN.
LIKE THE DEVIL THEY HAVE MANY NAMES:
CENTRISTS, MODERATES, CORPORATISTS.

TODAY JIMMY CARTER IS FONDLY
REMEMBERED FOR HIS SMILE, EASY MANNER,
AND HIS POST-PRESIDENTIAL WORK WITH
HABITAT FOR HUMANITY, HIS EFFORTS TO
MEDIATE CRISES IN THE MIDDLE EAST AND
HIS SUPPORT FOR LIBERAL CAUSES.

WHEN HIS DAUGHTER AMY GOT ARRESTED
WITH ABBIE HOFFMAN AT ANTIWAR
PROTESTS IN THE 1980s IN MASSACHUSETTS,
HE WAS SUPPORTIVE OF BOTH.

IT'S NEARLY LOST TO
HISTORY, BUT JIMMY
CARTER'S PRESIDENCY
MARKED THE FIRST
RIGHTWARD LURCH IN
MODERN DEMOCRATIC
POLITICS.

National Security Advisor Zbigniew Brzezinski and President Carter confer over the day's edition of the President's Daily Brief.

WHAT HISTORY CALLS THE "REAGAN DEFENSE BUILD-UP" OF THE 1980s ACTUALLY BEGAN UNDER CARTER.

CARTER BROUGHT BACK DRAFT REGISTRATION AND SIGNED A BILL SLAMMING REFUSENIKS WITH FIVE YEARS IN PRISON.

CARTER'S RESPONSE TO THE SOVIET INVASION OF AFGHANISTAN WAS APPALLING. NOT ONLY DID HE ARM AND FUND THE MUJAHIDEEN WHOSE PROGENY, AL QAEDA, WOULD CARRY OUT THE 9/11 ATTACKS ALMOST A QUARTER-CENTURY LATER, HE POLITICIZED THE OLYMPICS BY BOYCOTTING THE 1980 GAMES IN MOSCOW.

AND HE PROVOKED THE IRAN HOSTAGE CRISIS BY OFFERING REFUGE TO THE DEPOSED DICTATOR, THE CORRUPT SHAH OF IRAN.

IMPORTANTLY, CARTER WAS THE FIRST DEMOCRATIC PRESIDENT SINCE FDR NOT TO SIGN INTO LAW A SINGLE MAJOR ANTI-POVERTY PROGRAM.

HE DIDN'T EVEN TRY TO PROPOSE ONE.

Average Hourly Earnings of Production and Nonsupervisory E
Average Hourly Earnings of Production and Nonsupervisory E
Urban Consumers: All Items (right)

ATTEMPTS TO LIFT AMERICANS OUT OF POVERTY, FRONT AND CENTER ON DEMOCRATIC PLATFORMS SINCE 1932, WAS NO LONGER A PRIORITY AFTER CARTER WAS ELECTED. NEITHER WAS IMPROVING THE LOT OF MIDDLE-CLASS WORKERS.

| 1970 | 1975 | 1980 | 1985 | 1990 |

NO DEMOCRATIC PRESIDENT SINCE, NEITHER CLINTON NOR OBAMA, HAS EVEN FLOATED THE IDEA OF A FEDERAL PROGRAM TO ATTACK THE COUNTRY'S RAPIDLY WIDENING DISPARITY OF INCOME BETWEEN RICH AND POOR. NEITHER HAVE ANY OF THE NOMINEES WHO LOST.

STARTING IN THE 1970s SO-CALLED PROGRESSIVES (ONCE THE STALWARTS OF THE DEMOCRATIC PARTY) GOT PUSHED INTO AN ODD KIND OF POLITICAL WILDERNESS: WHILE NOMINALLY STILL TOLERATED WITHIN THE PARTY (ANYWAY, IN A TWO-PARTY DUOPOLY, WHERE ELSE COULD THEY GO?), THEY WERE RUTHLESSLY SHUNTED OUT OF PARTY LEADERSHIP ROLES.

"[Progressives] ran their candidates and tried to influence the platform. When they failed, they rallied behind the centrist candidate. Certainly the liberals have supported recent centrist candidates, starting with Jimmy Carter, with more loyalty than the conservatives showed to the candidacy of George McGovern. The 1992 campaign is a case in point. The liberal coalition—labor, environmentalists, minorities, fundamentalists, gays—were the shock troops of [Bill] Clinton's political army. They were the activists who knocked on doors, raised money, and organized precincts."

—Jeff Faux, *American Prospect*, 2001

AS SEEN WITH DONALD TRUMP'S TAKEOVER OF THE GOP, A PARTY'S PRESIDENTIAL STANDARD-BEARER SETS THE TONE AND POLICY AGENDA FOR THE IMMEDIATE FUTURE. DEMOCRATIC CENTRISTS WORKED TO MAKE CERTAIN THAT THE PARTY'S NOMINEES WERE ALWAYS ONE OF THEIR OWN, NEVER A PROGRESSIVE.

Hillary Clinton Targets Republicans Turned Off by Donald Trump

Obama says he'd be seen as moderate Republican in 1980s

BY IAN SWANSON - 12/14/12 11:49 AM EST

Democrats' Far-Left Lean Risks More Than the Presidency

COMMENTARY
By Mort Kondracke

Back to the Center, Democrats

By Mark Penn and Andrew Stein

July 6, 2017

Jimmy Carter cautions Democrats not to scare off moderates

By Bill Barrow   September 12, 2018

THE CENTRISTS BRANDED THEMSELVES AS "NEW DEMOCRATS": PRAGMATIC, SKEPTICAL OF IDENTITY POLITICS, DETERMINED TO WIN BACK THE "SILENT MAJORITY" DEMOCRATS WHO TURNED OUT FIRST FOR NIXON AND, IN 1980, EVEN MORE DECISIVELY FOR RONALD REAGAN.

ECONOMIC POPULISM WAS DEAD. THEY OPPOSED SINGLE-PAYER HEALTH CARE. THEY PUSHED FOR WELFARE REFORM THAT SOUNDED LIKE SOMETHING A HARD-RIGHT REPUBLICAN MIGHT HAVE DREAMED UP.

One of my cartoons from 1997

IDEOLOGICALLY, THESE "THIRD WAY" DEMOCRATS WERE LED BY THE DEMOCRATIC LEADERSHIP COUNCIL (DLC) FORMED IN 1985 FROM THE ASHES OF A SIMILAR GROUP CALLED THE COALITION FOR A DEMOCRATIC MAJORITY. MEMBERS INCLUDED GOVERNOR BILL CLINTON OF ARKANSAS, WHO STEPPED DOWN AS CHAIR WHEN HE ANNOUNCED HIS RUN FOR PRESIDENT IN 1992.

The Democrats

Clinton Says He's Not Leaning Left but Taking a New 'Third Way'

By MICHAEL KELLY
Special to The New York Times

BOSTON, Sept. 25 — Seeking to counter this week's Republican offensive portraying him as a leftist, tax-mad, big-government liberal, Bill Clinton today began an effort to once more position himself as a "third way" Democrat, neither of the left nor the right.

At the same time, the Democratic Presidential nominee sought depicting his opponent as a "ing" President who is "out of to of ideas and out of time," a clings to the "stale, failed rhe the past."

Mr. Clinton introduced his tense in a noontime address if almost preachly earnest to a crowd of invited guests at the U ty of Connecticut at Hartford, Hartford. He echoed it, in a fashion, before a passionate, young crowd of more than 10,00 packed shoulder-to-shoulder n historic Faneuil Hall here.

'A Can-Do Country'

"You cannot permit this ele be about false choices from An past, about the same old catego same old boxes we try to put

we had better seize them, and we had better be willing to park all this aimless hot-air rhetoric at the door and deal with the people's problems and the people's agenda.

"I think this is a can-do country," he continued. "This should not be an election about the stale, failed political rhetoric of the past. If we let this be about tax and spend and trickle-down, we ought to be ashamed of ourselves.

Candidates On Television
The Presidential campaigners have scheduled these television appearances in coming days:
President Bush

increases.

Clinton campaign officials said they decided it was imperative that the candidate directly and forcefully address Mr. Bush's attacks, and he did, in a speech that top operatives worked on over several days, only to have Mr. Clinton rewrite it this morning.

"George Bush says there is a Grand Canyon between us, and in that he is certainly right," the Governor said.

GOV. BILL CLINTON

In a speech yesterday at the University of Connecticut in West Hartford.

❝If and when Mr. Bush does actually debate me, he'll find that he's facing a different challenger, a different kind of Democrat who understands that the great issue of this election and our time is how we can help America in a global economy to build a society where the power of government is used to help people and to help the private sector create jobs and increase incomes, to solve problems like the health care crisis instead of just talk about them, and to do it in ways that promote more innovation and less bureaucracy, and finally to educate and empower people ... amily's futures.

... ate enterprise and ... is rhetoric and the ..., between his pro-

D'OH!

PRESIDENT CLINTON HAS APPOINTED A NEW REPUBLICAN CABINET TO WORK WITH THE REPUBLICAN CONGRESS TO PASS REPUBLICAN LEGISLATION... AGAIN.

BARACK OBAMA WAS NEVER OFFICIALLY A DLC MEMBER. BUT TWO MONTHS AFTER BECOMING PRESIDENT, OBAMA TOLD THE NEW DEMOCRAT COALITION THAT HE WAS A "NEW DEMOCRAT," "PRO-GROWTH DEMOCRAT," THAT HE "SUPPORT[ED] FREE AND FAIR TRADE," AND WAS "VERY CONCERNED ABOUT A RETURN TO PROTECTIONISM"—ALL DLC POSITIONS.

THOUGH TECHNICALLY NO LONGER AN ACTIVE ORGANIZATION, DLC AND "MAINSTREAM" (I.E., CORPORATIST, CENTRIST, MASS MEDIA-APPROVED) DEMOCRATIC PARTY IDEOLOGY ARE NOW VIRTUALLY INDISTINGUISHABLE.

THE TRIUMPH OF THE DLC DIDN'T COME EASY. IT REQUIRED BACKROOM DEALS, BREAKING RULES, AND UNDERMINING DEMOCRACY.

1980: LIBERAL ICON TED KENNEDY CHALLENGED INCUMBENT JIMMY CARTER FROM THE LEFT. KENNEDY WAS A SOLID AND UNCOMPROMISING PROGRESSIVE VOICE IN THE SENATE THROUGHOUT HIS CAREER, STANDING UP FOR ALL THE RIGHT CAUSES.

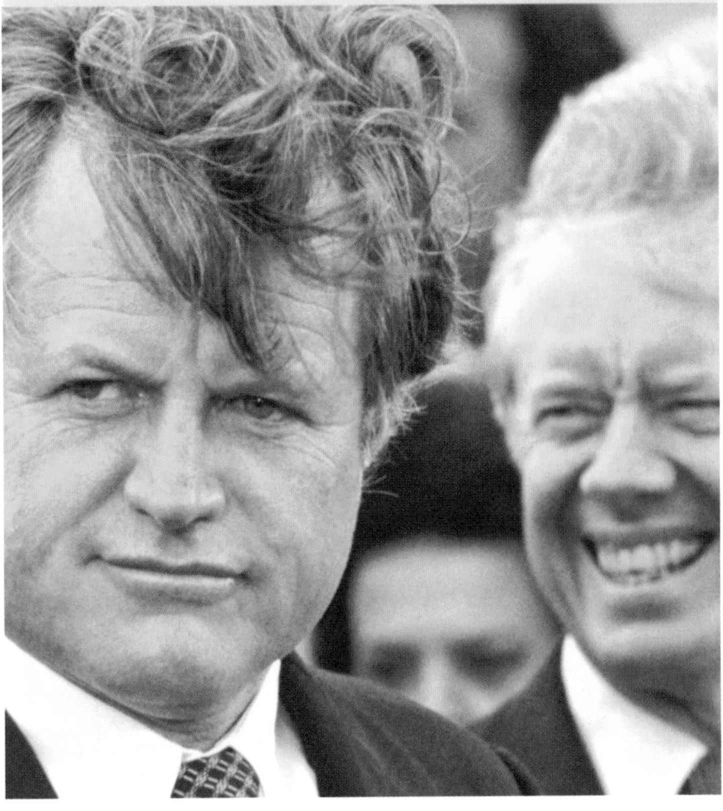

CARTER VS. KENNEDY WAS A BRUTAL FIGHT FOR THE SOUL OF THE DEMOCRATIC PARTY. AS THE HOSTAGE CRISIS DRAGGED ON IN IRAN, THE PRESIDENT WEAKENED EVEN MORE. KENNEDY HAD MOMENTUM.

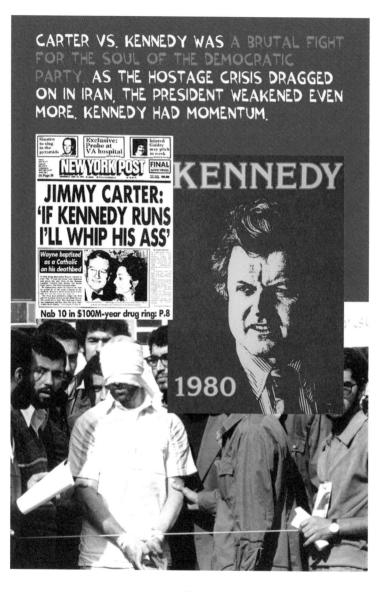

65

IN 1980 DELEGATES WERE STILL "UNBOUND," I.E., FREE TO VOTE FOR THE CANDIDATE OF THEIR CHOICE. THOUGH IT SEEMS STRANGE TODAY THAT PRIMARY VOTES WERE TREATED MERELY AS SUGGESTIONS, THE UNBOUND-DELEGATE RULE COULD PROVE TO BE SMART POLITICS.

IF THE CANDIDATE WITH THE MOST VOTES IN PRIMARIES HELD MONTHS EARLIER WERE TO BECOME LESS POPULAR—OR LESS PALATABLE TO THE POWERS THAT BE—AS THE CONVENTION DREW NEAR, IT ALLOWED FOR THE PARTY, LATE IN THE PRIMARIES PROCESS, TO PICK THE CANDIDATE IT WANTED TO GO WITH IN THE GENERAL ELECTION.

WHICH WAS EXACTLY THE SITUATION IN
1980. CARTER HAD AMASSED THE MOST
DELEGATES BUT KENNEDY WAS SURGING.

THAT SEEMED TO AUGUR A KENNEDY
VICTORY. BUT THE CENTRISTS STAGED A
COUP. IN WHAT WOULD BECOME THE LAST
TRULY EXCITING AND DRAMATIC POLITICAL
CONVENTION OF THE 20TH CENTURY,
CARTER'S FORCES—WHO CONTROLLED THE
DNC AND THUS THE CONVENTION HALL—
RAMMED THROUGH A CHANGE IN THE RULES.

Democrats Back Carter on Nomination Rule; Kennedy Withhdraws From Presidential Race

By HEDRICK SMITH

President Carter cleared his last obstacle to renomination last night with a surprisingly easy victory in the crucial fight over the rules of the Democratic

DELEGATES WOULD BE BOUND TO VOTE
ALONG WITH THEIR DISTRICTS. THAT GAVE
CARTER, SINKING IN THE POLLS, THE
NOMINATION.

"THE WORK GOES ON, THE CAUSE ENDURES,
THE HOPE STILL LIVES, AND THE
DREAM SHALL NEVER DIE."

— SENATOR EDWARD M KENNEDY

LET US CONTINUE HIS LEGACY OF FAITH IN THE PEOPLE
AND FAITH IN THE WORK THAT HAS YET TO BE DONE.

GO FORTH

This line from Kennedy's concession
speech at the 1980 convention is now
so iconic that it is routinely
commercialized.

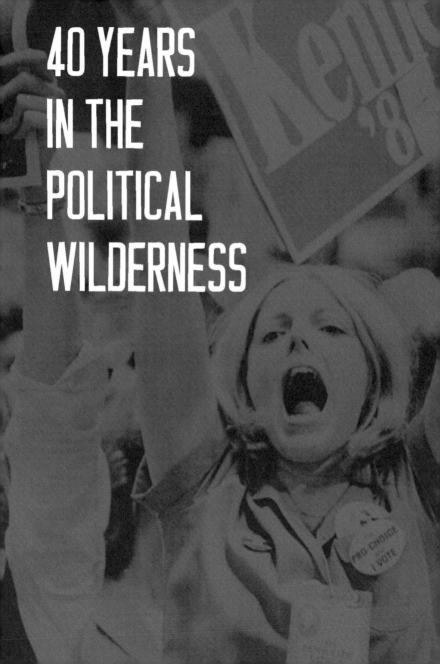

40 YEARS IN THE POLITICAL WILDERNESS

IT IS NOT MUCH DISCUSSED IN SCHOOLS OR REFERENCED IN PUNDITRY, BUT JUST A CENTURY AGO THE UNITED STATES HAD A VIBRANT SOCIALIST PARTY. ITS LEADER, EUGENE DEBS, WON 900,000 VOTES, NEARLY 6% OF THE POPULAR VOTE, IN 1912. (AND THAT WAS THE YEAR TEDDY ROOSEVELT RAN ON THE PROGRESSIVE "BULL MOOSE" TICKET, SO THE LEFTIST VOTE WAS DIVIDED.)

"While there is a lower class, I am in it, and while there is a criminal element, I am of it, and while there is a soul in prison, I am not free."

—Eugene Debs

TERRIFIED THAT REVOLUTION WOULD
COME TO THE U.S. AS IT HAD COME TO
RUSSIA, THE STATE SUPPRESSED THE
LEFT. DEBS WAS ARRESTED AND
IMPRISONED FOR THE "CRIME" OF
DISTRIBUTING LEAFLETS OPPOSING THE
UNITED STATES' INVOLVEMENT IN WORLD
WAR I IN EUROPE.

RULING AGAINST DEBS, SUPREME COURT JUSTICE OLIVER WENDELL HOLMES THUNDERED THAT ADVOCATING PEACE DURING WARTIME WAS TANTAMOUNT TO "SHOUTING FIRE IN A CROWDED THEATER." TODAY THE PHRASE IS UNDERSTOOD TO MEAN THAT FREEDOM OF SPEECH HAS LIMITS.

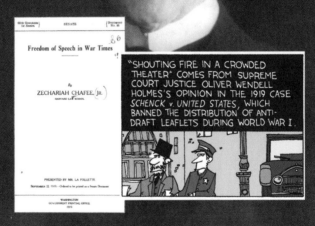

"SHOUTING FIRE IN A CROWDED THEATER" COMES FROM SUPREME COURT JUSTICE OLIVER WENDELL HOLMES'S OPINION IN THE 1919 CASE *SCHENCK v. UNITED STATES*, WHICH BANNED THE DISTRIBUTION OF ANTI-DRAFT LEAFLETS DURING WORLD WAR I.

ACTUALLY, HOLMES LATER REVERSED HIS OWN RULING AND RELEASED DEBS. SO, YOU ACTUALLY DO HAVE THE RIGHT TO SHOUT FIRE IN A CROWDED THEATER.

THE GOVERNMENT WENT AFTER MARXIST-
ORIENTED LEFTISM VIA THE FBI'S PALMER
RAIDS, SHOW TRIALS LIKE THAT OF THE
ANARCHISTS SACCO AND VANZETTI IN
THE 1920s AND THE McCARTHYITE RED
SCARE AND HOLLYWOOD BLACKLIST OF
THE 1950s. COMMUNISTS AND SOCIALISTS
LEARNED TO SHUT UP ABOUT THEIR
POLITICAL CONVICTIONS.

The New York Times

NEW YORK, SATURDAY, JANUARY 3, 1920.   TWO CENTS

REDS RAIDED IN SCORES OF CITIES;
2,600 ARRESTS, 700 IN NEW YORK;
DEPORTATION HEARINGS BEGIN TODAY

RAIDS ON 13 CENTRES HERE

Federal Officers Seize
Hundreds of Reds at
Their Meeting Places.

MANY MIR PAPERS SEIZED

Raiders Ordered to Make Cleanup Thorough,
Warned Against Violence or Taking Valuables

RAID FROM COAST TO COAST

Secret Service Men
Make Simultaneous
Swoop.

PREPARING FOR SIX MONTHS

SATURDAY EVENING, JAN

DEPORTATION PROB

NETTE

Federal Agen

4,500 ARRESTED
NATION-WIDE DR
ROUNDUP CONTI

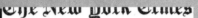

PALMER DECLARES
ALIEN 'REDS' ARE
TO BE DEPORTED

Determined and Prompt Action Will Be Taken
Against Radicals Caught in Widespread Clean-

BEGINNING IN 1932, HOWEVER, FDR'S
DEMOCRATIC PARTY MADE SPACE FOR
VOTERS AND CANDIDATES INTERESTED IN
IMPROVING THE LOT OF THE AVERAGE
PERSON AS LONG AS THEIR APPROACH
TO CAPITALISM WAS REFORMIST RATHER
THAN REVOLUTIONARY.

AND THAT SET OF BELIEFS DOMINATED
DEMOCRATIC PARTY POLITICS AND LED
TO ONE OF THE GREATEST ECONOMIC
REVOLUTIONS IN RECORDED HISTORY, THE
POSTWAR RISE OF THE AMERICAN MIDDLE
CLASS.

THE DEFEAT OF CARTER MARKED THE RISE OF THE "REAGAN REVOLUTION," A BRASH NEW SELF-CONFIDENT BRAND OF HARD-CORE CONSERVATIVE REPUBLICANISM.

THE FORMER B-MOVIE ACTOR AND RIGHT-WING CALIFORNIA GOVERNOR SLASHED THE BUDGET OF EDUCATION AND WELFARE PROGRAMS, AND CUT TAXES FOR THE WEALTHY AND BIG BUSINESS UNDER THE DOCTRINE OF "TRICKLE-DOWN ECONOMICS."

A PROGRAM HANDING OUT
GOVERNMENT-SURPLUS
CHEESE WAS THE
ARCHETYPAL FACE OF A
HEARTLESS ADMINISTRATION
THAT EVICTED THE MENTALLY
ILL ONTO CITY STREETS.

Surplus Cheese Goes to Poor As President Signs Farm Bill

WASHINGTON, Dec. 22 (AP) — President Reagan signed into law a four-year, $11 billion farm support bill today, then gave poor Americans a holiday slice of the cheese surplus piled in Government warehouses.

Mr. Reagan's signature on the farm

quate and critics for some farmers others. The bill pa 203, last Wednesda voting no.

In Congression members from t

NEW YORK

Reagan's Homeless

THE LEFT CONTINUED ITS TRADITION OF
STREET-LEVEL ACTIVISM UNDER
REAGANISM. BUT 1960s TACTICS WERE NO
LONGER EFFECTIVE. A UNION-BACKED
"SOLIDARITY DAY" RALLY DREW
HUNDREDS OF THOUSANDS TO THE
WASHINGTON MALL TO PROTEST
REAGAN'S FIRING OF UNIONIZED AIR
TRAFFIC CONTROLLERS AND
DEMONSTRATE AGAINST REAGANISM IN
GENERAL.

THE GROUP ACT UP ORGANIZED
SENSATIONAL STUNTS OF RESISTANCE
TO CALL ATTENTION TO THE HIV/AIDS
CRISIS, AND THE GOVERNMENT REFUSAL
TO FUND RESEARCH. PUNK ROCKERS HELD
"ROCK AGAINST REAGAN" CONCERTS.
NOTHING HELPED.

WITHIN THE RANKS OF ACTIVISTS, THERE
WAS A SENSE OF MALAISE AND A RISING
AWARENESS THAT THEIR TACTICS WERE
NO LONGER EFFECTIVE.

THE GOVERNMENT SIMPLY DIDN'T CARE
ANYMORE. PROTEST MARCHES BECAME
FEWER AND FARTHER BETWEEN. AS THE
GOP MOVED EVER FURTHER TO THE RIGHT,
THE DEMOCRATIC PARTY DRIFTED RIGHT
IN EMULATION OF REPUBLICANS AND TO
COURT LOBBYIST DOLLARS FOR THEIR
CAMPAIGN COFFERS.

THE WANING OF STREET DEMONSTRATIONS LEFT ELECTORAL POLITICS AS THE MAIN WAY TO DEFEND THE LIBERAL GAINS OF THE POST-FDR ERA. AGITATING FOR SOLUTIONS TO NEW PROBLEMS SEEMED TOO AMBITIOUS. LIBERALS TRIED TO WORK WITHIN A DEMOCRATIC PARTY INCREASINGLY DOMINATED BY MODERATES WITH A DLC MINDSET.

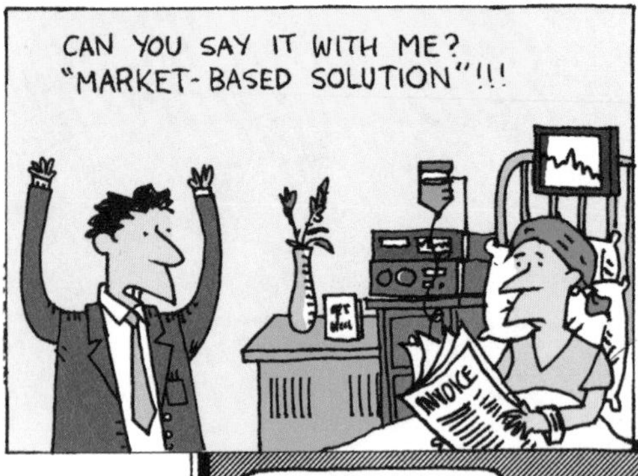
CAN YOU SAY IT WITH ME? "MARKET-BASED SOLUTION"!!!
INVOICE

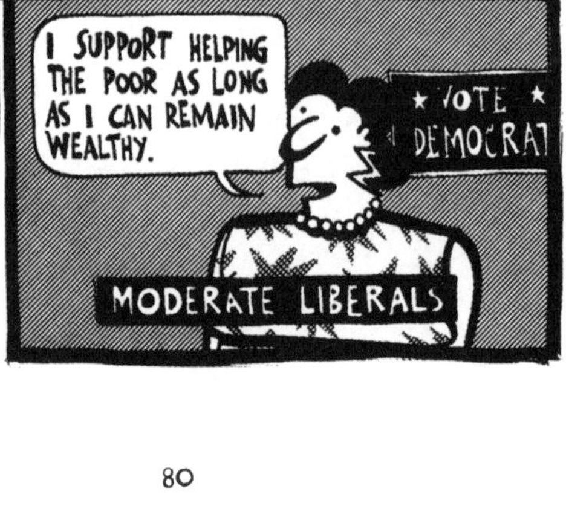
I SUPPORT HELPING THE POOR AS LONG AS I CAN REMAIN WEALTHY.
★ VOTE ★
DEMOCRAT
MODERATE LIBERALS

THE TWO-PARTY TRAP WAS NEVER MORE APPARENT THAN DURING THIS PERIOD. IF PROGRESSIVES VOTED THIRD PARTY OR ABSTAINED FROM VOTING, RIGHT-WING REPUBLICANS WON MORE ELECTIONS. IF THEY VOTED DEMOCRATIC, THEIR VOTE WAS TAKEN FOR GRANTED.

MOST PROGRESSIVES STUCK WITH THE PARTY. BUT IT WAS A MUG'S GAME AND THEY KNEW IT.

MEANWHILE, IN ONE ELECTION AFTER ANOTHER, FROM LOCAL RACES FOR CITY COUNCIL AND MAYOR, CONSERVATIVES BUILT ON THEIR VICTORIES AND PUSHED THE REPUBLICAN PARTY EVEN FURTHER TO THE RIGHT.

DEMOCRATIC PARTY LEADERS FACED A CHOICE: STAKE OUT A CLEAR ALTERNATIVE BY DEFENDING TRADITIONAL PROGRESSIVE VALUES, OR TRY TO PEEL AWAY "SWING" VOTERS FROM THE GOP BY ESPOUSING MORE CENTRIST POSITIONS. NO ONE EVEN DREAMED AN AGGRESSIVELY LEFT CANDIDATE COULD GET ANYWHERE ON THE NATIONAL STAGE.

PARTY LEADERS WERE PREDISPOSED TOWARD MODERATION. ADDING TO THE POLITICAL PRESSURE FROM THE RIGHT WAS A NEWS MEDIA UNDERGOING CORPORATE CONSOLIDATION, HIRING FEWER WORKING-CLASS JOURNALISTS IN FAVOR OF JOURNALISM-SCHOOL GRADUATES WHO WERE CHILDREN OF THE RULING ELITES. EDITORIAL PAGES MOVED RIGHT AS WELL. PROGRESSIVE OPINION WRITERS WERE GOING EXTINCT.

The 30 Biggest Political Donors on the Fortune 500
Political Donations Between the Years 2007 and 2017

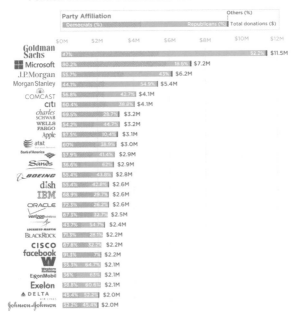

	Party Affiliation		Others (%)
	Democrats (%)	Republicans (%)	Total donations ($)

Goldman Sachs	47%	52.2%	$11.5M
Microsoft	80.2%	18.0%	$7.2M
J.P.Morgan	55.7%	43%	$6.2M
Morgan Stanley	44.1%	54.9%	$5.4M
COMCAST	56.8%	42.7%	$4.1M
citi	60.4%	38.8%	$4.1M
charles SCHWAB	69.5%	28.7%	$3.2M
WELLS FARGO	54.2%	44.7%	$3.2M
Apple	87.5%	10.4%	$3.1M
at&t	60%	38.9%	$3.0M
Bank of America	57.9%	41.4%	$2.9M
Sands	36.6%	62%	$2.9M
BOEING	55.4%	43.8%	$2.8M
dish	55.4%	42.8%	$2.6M
IBM	68.9%	29.7%	$2.6M
ORACLE	72.3%	26.2%	$2.6M
verizon wireless	67.3%	32.7%	$2.5M
	43.7%	54.7%	$2.4M
BLACKROCK	71.3%	28.1%	$2.2M
CISCO	67.8%	32.2%	$2.2M
facebook	91.4%	7%	$2.2M
Western Refining	35.3%	64.7%	$2.1M
ExxonMobil	36%	63%	$2.1M
Exelon	38.8%	60.6%	$2.1M
DELTA AIR LINES	45.4%	52.2%	$2.0M
Johnson&Johnson	52.2%	45.4%	$2.0M

$0M $2M $4M $6M $8M $10M $12M

A NEW FUND-RAISING MODEL EMERGED. AS LABOR UNIONS SHRANK IN SIZE AND INFLUENCE, DEMOCRATS TURNED TO WALL STREET AND BIG CORPORATIONS FOR CAMPAIGN DONATIONS. BIG DONORS EXPECTED AND RECEIVED CONSIDERATION WHEN DEMOCRATS DRAFTED OR COSPONSORED LEGISLATION.

RONALD REAGAN'S FIRST TERM WAS
MARRED BY CONTROVERSY AND A
RECESSION THAT LEFT MILLIONS OF
AMERICANS UNEMPLOYED AND
UNDERERPLOYED.

YET A RUDDERLESS DEMOCRATIC PARTY
WAS UNABLE TO CAPITALIZE ON THE
PRESIDENT'S WEAKNESSES. FORMER VICE
PRESIDENT WALTER MONDALE, THE LAST
TRADITIONAL DEMOCRATIC LIBERAL
NOMINEE, LOST BY A 59% TO 41%
LANDSLIDE.

85

IN A NOW-OBSCURE EPISODE, CIVIL RIGHTS
ACTIVIST JESSE JACKSON BUILT ON HIS
DRY-RUN PRIMARY CAMPAIGN FOUR
YEARS EARLIER TO COME OUT SWINGING
AGAINST THE PASSIVE, APOLOGETIC, AND
WEASELLY MICHAEL DUKAKIS, WHO HAD
BEEN PICKED BY PARTY BOSSES IN 1988.

"[I want] to bring justice in our land, mitigate misery in the world and bring peace on earth. Only in America is such a dream possible."

—The Rev. Jesse Jackson

Result Clouds the Race Among Democrats — Gephardt Finishes 3d

By R. W. APPLE Jr.
Special to The New York Times

DETROIT, March 26 — The Rev. Jesse Jackson dealt a blow to the Presidential candidacy of Gov. Michael S. Dukakis today, trouncing him in the popular vote in Michigan's Democratic caucuses and denying him the momentum he had sought in this big industrial state.

Despite an all-out effort, Representative Richard A. Gephardt of Missouri finished third. He said he would meet with his family on Sunday to decide

LOOKING BACK, JACKSON'S ACHIEVEMENT WAS REMARKABLE. JACKSON RECEIVED 6.9 MILLION VOTES AND WON 11 CONTESTS: SEVEN PRIMARIES (ALABAMA, THE DISTRICT OF COLUMBIA, GEORGIA, LOUISIANA, MISSISSIPPI, PUERTO RICO, AND VIRGINIA) AND FIVE CAUCUSES (ALASKA, DELAWARE, MICHIGAN, SOUTH CAROLINA, AND VERMONT). FOR A MOMENT, AFTER HE WON THE MICHIGAN CAUCUS, JACKSON HAD MORE PLEDGED DELEGATES THAN ALL THE OTHER CANDIDATES PUT TOGETHER.

THE SUCCESS OF JACKSON'S CAMPAIGN
DEMONSTRATED THE CONTINUING
APPETITE FOR PROGRESSIVISM WITHIN
PARTY RANKS. HE PROPOSED A NEW
WPA-STYLE FEDERAL HIRING PROGRAM,
SINGLE-PAYER HEALTH CARE,
REPARATIONS TO THE DESCENDANTS OF
SLAVES, AN INDEPENDENT PALESTINIAN
STATE, AND A 15% CUT TO THE
PENTAGON BUDGET.

"OUR NATION'S LEADERS MUST NOT BE ALLOWED TO HOLD A DOVE IN ONE HAND, A MISSILE IN THE OTHER."

Jesse L. Jackson

JESSE JACKSON, A VOTE TO STOP THE ARMS RACE

☑ JESSE JACKSON - THE ONLY CANDIDATE TO CALL FOR CUTTING THE DEFENSE BUDGET.

Since 1980 the military budget has grown 60% in real terms while our cities crumble. We will send $1.9 trillion to the Pentagon between 1982 and 1986 while our people go hungry and homeless. The military budget drains our ~~~~~~~~ources needed to rebuild our indus-~~~~~~~ home. MONDALE, HART ~~~~~~LL FOR RAISING THE ~~~~~N FURTHER: Jackson ~~~~~ -- a $60 billion cut.

~~~~ ONLY CANDI-~~~~IRST USE OF

~~~~g our government to ~~~ use nuclear weapons ~~~ the arms race; a prom-~~~ accidental nuclear war. ~~~ANDIDATE CALLING ~~~t and Mondale have both ~~~rst use of nuclear weapons.

☑ JESSE JACKSON - THE ONLY CANDIDATE TO CALL FOR A NEW FOREIGN POLICY -- PEACE IN CENTRAL AMERICA, PEACE IN THE MIDEAST.

From Viet Nam to El Salvador both Republicans and Democrats have voted to send our bombs and our children abroad to kill and be killed. We have had a foreign policy based on military might, protecting dictators and death squads, risking war around the world. Jesse Jackson is the only candidate calling for a new foreign policy based on mutual aid, respect and bold initiatives for peace. Mondale calls for a continued U.S. presence in Central and South America and in the Mideast to fight communism and protect U.S. interests -- arguments that got us into Viet Nam. Both Hart and Mondale call for building up our conventional and interventionary forces. A VOTE FOR JESSE JACKSON IS A VOTE TO STOP OUR WAR POLICIES AND BEGIN A PEACE POLICY.

The security we profess to seek in foreign adventures we will lose in our decaying cities. The bombs in Viet Nam explode at home. They destroy the hopes and possibilities for a decent America.
-- Dr. Martin Luther King, Jr., 1967

Justice at home and peace abroad. These are the themes of my campaign. I believe they are one great theme. When we promote a just, fair foreign policy, we will not be running the risk of foreign wars in third world "hot spots." We will not be embroiling ourselves in conflicts with people seeking justice. We will not need Gary Hart's "smaller more maneuverable battle ships" or Walter Mondale's

stealth bombers and midgetman missiles. We can cut our defense budget. We can invest the savings in our economy, our youth and our cities. We can train our youth to end the slums and rebuild the cities.

We can make our nation more just and more secure.

-- Jesse Jackson, 1984

☑ A STRONG VOTE FOR JESSE JACKSON WILL GIVE THE PEACE MOVEMENT A CHANCE TO SHAPE THE PLATFORM OF THE DEMOCRATIC PARTY

THIS HISTORIC RUN BY THE FIRST
NATIONALLY VIABLE AFRICAN AMERICAN
PRESIDENTIAL CANDIDATE WAS STYMIED
BY FORCES THAT WOULD BECOME
FAMILIAR TO ANY PROGRESSIVE WHO
TRIED TO CHALLENGE THE CENTRISTS'
GRIP ON THE DEMOCRATIC PARTY.

SEVERAL STATES JACKSON WON
AWARDED DELEGATES BY
CONGRESSIONAL DISTRICT,
SHORTCHANGING HIM IN THE DELEGATE
COUNT. THE DNC ALSO APPOINTED A
LOT OF SUPERDELEGATES, MOST OF
WHOM SUPPORTED DUKAKIS OVER
JACKSON.

JESSE JACKSON HAS BEEN WHITEWASHED FROM THE HISTORY OF THE DEMOCRATIC PARTY.

WHEN BARACK OBAMA BECAME THE FIRST AFRICAN AMERICAN NOMINEE OF A MAJOR PARTY AND THEN WAS ELECTED PRESIDENT, JESSE JACKSON WAS IGNORED AND TOLD TO STAY HOME RATHER THAN JOIN HIM ON THE CAMPAIGN TRAIL.

WHEN YOU CONSIDER ITS
LESS-THAN-STELLAR SUCCESS
RATE—OVER THE LAST FOUR DECADES,
WE'VE ONLY ELECTED TWO DEMOCRATIC
PRESIDENTS FOR A TOTAL OF 16 YEARS
IN OFFICE—THE DLC CHOKEHOLD OVER
THE DEMOCRATIC LEADERSHIP IS
REMARKABLE. ITS FIRST SUCCESS TOOK
AT LEAST 12 YEARS TO ACHIEVE: BILL
CLINTON.

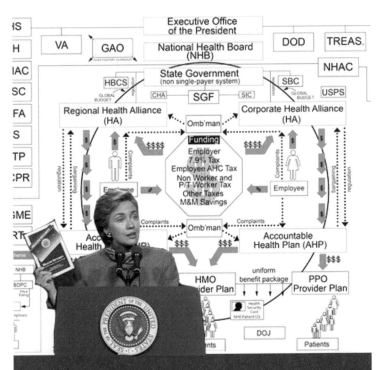

CLINTON PLAYED A DEMOCRAT ON TV. BUT YOU COULDN'T TELL BY HIS LEGISLATIVE AGENDA, MUCH LESS HIS ACHIEVEMENTS. HIS WIFE HILLARY'S STAB AT HEALTH CARE REFORM WAS AN EARLY VERSION OF THE OBAMA-ERA AFFORDABLE CARE ACT; IT WAS MAINLY DESIGNED TO PROTECT INSURANCE COMPANY PROFITS.

IN THE END CLINTON HAD JUST A FEW THINGS
TO SHOW FOR HIS TIME IN OFFICE: THE
JOBS-KILLING NORTH AMERICAN FREE TRADE
AGREEMENT AND THE PRO-BUSINESS WORLD
TRADE ORGANIZATION WERE BOTH
ORIGINALLY CONCEIVED OF BY RIGHT-WING
THINK TANKS. A CRIMINAL REFORM BILL
INCREASED PENALTIES AND TOSSED YOUNG
MEN OF COLOR INTO PRISON. CLINTON
ENDED "WELFARE AS WE KNOW IT," THROWING
MILLIONS OF PEOPLE LIVING JUST ABOVE THE
POVERTY LINE ONTO THE STREETS.

CLINTON'S VICE PRESIDENT, AL GORE, PRESENTED HIS 2000 CHALLENGE TO GEORGE W. BUSH AS SOMETHING JUST SHORT OF EXISTENTIAL.

GORE WOULD NOT HAVE INVADED IRAQ. HE UNDERSTOOD THE GRAVE THREAT TO THE ENVIRONMENT, AND HE WOULD HAVE FOUGHT HARD TO REVERSE CLIMATE CHANGE AND PROMOTE ALTERNATIVE SOURCES OF ENERGY.

BUT HE WOULDN'T HAVE STOOD UP TO CORPORATE POWER.

AL GORE: THE FIRST FOUR YEARS

2001 — IN AN EFFORT TO REACH BIPARTISANSHIP, I'VE APPOINTED 2 REPUBLICANS—TOM RIDGE AND TOMMY THOMPSON—TO MY CABINET.

2002 — THIS TAX CUT IS A BIT TOO GENEROUS TO THE RICH, BUT I HAD TO COMPROMISE WITH THE REPUBLICAN CONGRESS.

2003 — JUST BECAUSE MOST PEOPLE THINK NAFTA IS A DISASTER DOESN'T MEAN WE SHOULD REPEAL IT... AFTER ALL, CEOs THINK IT'S GREAT!

2004 — I NEED FOUR MORE YEARS TO KEEP FIGHTING FOR DEMOCRATIC VALUES!

RE-ELECT GORE FOR PENN'S

Tipper STILL Rocks!

AFTER DECADES OF BEING TOLD THAT OUR PRIORITIES DIDN'T MATTER, THAT WE NEEDED TO FALL IN LINE AND VOTE DEMOCRATIC WITHOUT ANY OF OUR POLICY PRIORITIES BEING PROMOTED, PROGRESSIVES WERE GETTING RESTLESS.

MANY PEOPLE COULDN'T SEE MUCH DIFFERENCE BETWEEN DEMOCRATIC AND REPUBLICAN PRESIDENTS.

NO MATTER WHO WON, THE COUNTRY KEPT MOVING RIGHT.

THIS SET THE STAGE FOR THE INDEPENDENT, INSURGENT CAMPAIGN OF LONG-TIME ATTORNEY AND CONSUMER ADVOCATE RALPH NADER. NADER RAN A WRITE-IN CAMPAIGN IN 1992 AND RAN AS THE GREEN PARTY PRESIDENTIAL CANDIDATE IN 1996.

HE CAUGHT FIRE IN 2000 RUNNING AGAIN AS THE GREEN PARTY CANDIDATE.

DEPARTING FROM LIBERAL ORTHODOXY,
YET FIRMLY IN KEEPING WITH HIS LONG-
STANDING PRINCIPLES, NADER RAN A
CAMPAIGN FOCUSED ON THE ELEPHANT IN
THE ROOM, ALBEIT ONE THAT NEITHER
PARTY NOR THE MEDIA WAS WILLING TO
TALK ABOUT AT THE TIME: CORPORATE
POWER IN OUR POLITICAL SYSTEM THAT
MADE BOTH DEMOCRATS AND
REPUBLICANS BEHOLDEN TO EVERYONE
EXCEPT THE PEOPLE.

Al Gore and George W. Bush are "tweedledee
and tweedledum—they look and act the same, so
it doesn't matter which you get."
—Ralph Nader, 2000

LIKE TED KENNEDY AND JESSE JACKSON BEFORE HIM, RALPH NADER POSED A CLEAR THREAT TO THE HEGEMONY OF THE CENTRISTS. THE DIRTY TRICKS CAME BACK OUT OF THE BAG:

BALLOT ACCESS WAS CHALLENGED BY THE DEMOCRATIC PARTY MACHINE IN STATE AFTER STATE. NADER'S POLITICAL MESSAGE WAS SILENCED IN THE MAJOR MEDIA.

JUNE 22, 2000

Nader Left Out of Media Websites

FAIR

Nader is absent from the list of possible candidates.

he is excluded

bers of the national press corps. From his February announcement through mid-October, Nader was practically invisible in the popular media. He called it a "media blackout," observing that six large multina-

Media Advisory / Hearing Scheduled for Ralph Nader N.C. Ballot Access Case

July 25, 2000

Nader Blocked at Debate Door

THE COMMISSION ON PRESIDENTIAL
DEBATES, AN ENTITY RUN BY THE
DEMOCRATS AND THE REPUBLICANS,
BLOCKED NADER FROM PARTICIPATING.
EVEN WHEN HE ATTEMPTED TO ATTEND
AS A SPECTATOR, HE WAS REFUSED
ENTRY.

I INTERVIEWED NADER THE AFTERNOON OF MARCH 14, 2019. HE WAS RUNNING LATE BECAUSE HE HAD JUST GOTTEN A TERRIBLE PHONE CALL. HIS GREAT NIECE HAD DIED.

HE WAS SHAKEN.

SHE WAS ON THE SECOND BOEING 737 MAX 8 PLANE CRASH, THE ONE IN ETHIOPIA.

SAMYA STUMO WAS 24.

EVER THE CONSUMER ADVOCATE, NADER
ZEROED IN ON THE CORPORATE GREED AND
CORNER-CUTTING THAT CONTRIBUTED TO
THE TRAGIC DEATHS OF STUMO AND
HUNDREDS OF OTHER PASSENGERS ON THE
ETHIOPIAN AIRLINES AND LION AIR FLIGHTS
THAT CRASHED DUE TO A DESIGN FLAW
CAUSED BY BOEING'S ATTEMPT TO SAVE
MONEY.

"If we don't get this right, if we don't end the
cozy relationship between the patsy FAA, the
captured agency, which has been documented
for years, and the Boeing company, 5,000 of
these fatally flawed planes will be in the air all
over the world with millions of passengers."
—Ralph Nader

SAD AND ANGRY, NADER AND I TURNED THE CONVERSATION TOWARD HIS EXPERIENCE RUNNING FOR PRESIDENT OUTSIDE THE CONFINES OF THE DEMOCRATIC-REPUBLICAN DUOPOLY.

"It's easier to take over the Democratic Party than to run on a third-party ticket because the Electoral College stands in the way. [Ross] Perot got 19% of the vote but zero Electoral College votes in 1992. There's no other country in the world that has such a stranglehold on the democratic process. Then a viable third party has to suddenly become massive immediately because otherwise it will be plagued by accusations that it's a 'spoiler.'"

"It's completely unnatural. When nature produces a seed it gives it a chance to sprout. What if nature suddenly said, we're not going to recognize any seed that doesn't suddenly turn into an oak tree?"

WHAT, I WANTED TO KNOW, STOPS A THIRD PARTY FROM TAKING ROOT IN OUR SYSTEM?

"Because it's ingrained in us in high school. Remember *Scholastic* magazine? At election time, they only offer two choices. Right from the beginning, people understand that third parties can't win. Why are you trying this? You're not going to get any coverage, reporters tell you, because you can't win."

Two Parties

- The two major political parties are
  - Democrats = more liberal
  - Republicans = more conservative

WE TALKED ABOUT BERNIE SANDERS'S PROSPECTS IN THE 2020 CAMPAIGN. AS A SELF-DESCRIBED "DEMOCRATIC SOCIALIST," HE WOULD SURELY BE ATTACKED FOR FAVORING SOCIALISM.

"Socialism is government ownership of the means of production. Capitalism is corporate ownership of the means of government. This is social-democratic stuff, middle of the road for Western Europe. What's the big deal? Pensions, paid vacation, higher minimum wage, universal health care, tuition-free higher education, clean parks, inexpensive public transit, stronger labor union laws. That's real radical."

I ASKED: IS THERE HOPE?

"There is hope. It takes one percent of the people to make change. Name one major social-justice movement in our country that required more than one percent. If we can't get one out of 100 adults to do the right thing as seen by a majority of the 100 adults, there's no hope for this country. We're talking 2.5 million people. If I had the support of one billionaire, I could make it happen in six months."

"How can you be a centrist and support positions that are not supported by a majority of the people? Leftists are supporting positions that are overwhelmingly supported, like the Fight for Fifteen [dollars an hour minimum wage]. The press is very culpable in promoting these nomenclatures that are nonsense. People like Biden like to call themselves centrists and so they're called centrists in the media. What's so centrist about supporting the Iraq War? What's so centrist about supporting NAFTA and the WTO?"

I LEFT NADER'S OFFICE THINKING: WHAT KIND OF COUNTRY IS THIS THAT THIS MAN, WHO SPEAKS SO MUCH SENSE, IS MARGINALIZED AND OSTRACIZED AS A "SPOILER" BY POLITICAL ENEMIES AND JOURNALISTS WHO ARE CONSISTENTLY WRONG?

"When I was out on the road, I had a lot to say, but the mainstream press didn't cover any of it. The campus papers or the small newspapers did."
—Ralph Nader

The Thistle

Volume 13, Number 2; Sept./Oct., 2000

Nader Holds Biggest Rally of His Campaign in Minnesota

The Target Center sports arena in Minneapolis was filled by more than 12000 people last Friday night, paying $7 each to hear the Green Party presidential candidate Ralph Nader denounce the major party candidates and call for social justice.

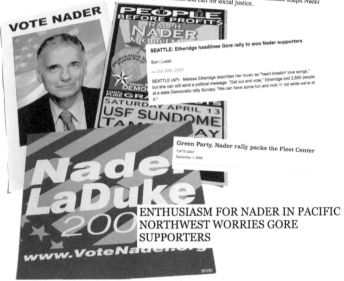

SEATTLE: Etheridge headlines Gore rally to woo Nader supporters

Sun | Local

— Oct 30th, 2000

SEATTLE (AP) - Melissa Etheridge describes her music as "heart-breakin' love songs," but she can still send a political message. "Get out and vote," Etheridge told 2,800 people at a state Democratic rally Sunday. "We can have some fun and rock 'n' roll while we're at it."

Green Party, Nader rally packs the Fleet Center

TUFTS DAILY
September 1, 2000

ENTHUSIASM FOR NADER IN PACIFIC NORTHWEST WORRIES GORE SUPPORTERS

TO THIS DAY, MANY DEMOCRATS
FOLLOW THE LEAD OF THE MAINSTREAM
MEDIA BY CALLING NADER A "SPOILER" IN
2000. THE ACCUSATION THAT HE TOOK
VOTES AWAY FROM GORE AND
THEREFORE BEARS RESPONSIBILITY FOR
THE BUSH PRESIDENCY RELIES ON AN
UNDEMOCRATIC ASSUMPTION: ONLY THE
DEMOCRATIC AND REPUBLICAN PARTIES
ARE LEGITIMATE AND, BY EXTENSION, ALL
OTHER IDEAS DO NOT OR SHOULD NOT
MATTER.

Ralph Nader Was Indispensable To The Republican Party

Nader Elected Bush: Why We Shouldn't Forget

Nader's Traitors

Ralph Nader regrets rien

No, Ralph Nader Did Not Hand the 2000 Presidential Election to George W. Bush

More than 12 times as many Florida Democrats rejected Al Gore in favor of Bush than they did for Nader.

ANTHONY FISHER | 8.3.2016 8:45 AM

THE SPOILER MEME IS A SMEAR. STUDIES
PROVE THAT NADER'S SUPPORT DID NOT
DRAW FROM VOTERS WHO OTHERWISE
WOULD HAVE VOTED DEMOCRATIC MORE
THAN FROM THOSE WHO OTHERWISE
WOULD HAVE VOTED REPUBLICAN. HE DID
NOT COST GORE THE ELECTION, OR EVEN
THE STATE OF FLORIDA.

Politics

• E-mail this story • Subscribe to the newspaper • Sign-up for e-mail news

05/11/2001 - Updated 10:36 AM ET

Revisiting the Florida vote: Final tally

INTERACTIVE
GRAPHIC
✓Click here

Florida voter errors cost Gore the election

By Dennis Cauchon and Jim Drinkard, USA TODAY

George W. Bush would have won a hand recount of all disputed ballots in Florida's presidential election if the most widely accepted standard for judging votes had been applied, the first comprehensive examination of the ballots shows. However, the review of 171,908 ballots also reveals that voting mistakes by thousands of Democratic voters — errors that legally disqualified their ballots — probably cost former vice president Al Gore 15,000 to 25,000 votes. That's enough to have decisively won Florida and the White House. Gore's best chance to win was lost before the ballots were counted, the study shows. Voters' confusion with ballot instruction and design and voting machines appears to have changed the course of U.S. history.

Who won Florida?

Who would have won if Al Gore had gotten the manual counts he requested in four counties?
Answer: George W. Bush.

Who would have won if the U.S. Supreme Court had not stopped the hand recount of undervotes, which are ballots that registered no machine-readable vote for president?
Answer: Bush, under 3 of 4 standards.

Who would have won if all disputed ballots - including those rejected by machines because they had more than one vote for president - had been recounted by hand?
Answer: Bush, under the 2 most widely used standards; Gore, under the 2 least used.

Who does it appear most voters intended to vote for?
Answer: Gore.

THOUGH BASELESS, THE ANTI-NADER NARRATIVE LIVES ON BECAUSE IT SERVES MULTIPLE PURPOSES. IT RETROACTIVELY VALIDATES AL GORE'S DLC-STYLE CENTRIST CAMPAIGN PLATFORM, WHICH PROGRESSIVES DID NOT SUPPORT. IT'S A CUDGEL USED TO DISCOURAGE FAITHLESS DEMOCRATS FROM FORMING A THIRD PARTY.

NADER SERVES AS AN ILLUSTRATION OF WHAT HAPPENS TO YOU WHEN YOU CHALLENGE THE MODERATE STATUS QUO: THEY PILLORY YOU, THEY SMEAR YOU, THEY BLAME YOU FOR THEIR OWN SINS.

AFTER GORE DECIDED NOT TO RUN AGAIN
IN 2004, VERMONT GOVERNOR HOWARD
DEAN LAUNCHED ANOTHER GREAT
PROGRESSIVE HOPE CAMPAIGN.

"Nearly 1 in 10 retired
people have had to return to
the workforce because they
have lost their pensions.
Young people returning
home to live with their
parents after graduation
because they can't find a job.
Companies leaving the
country to avoid paying
taxes, or avoid paying people
a livable wage."

HE CAME OUT SWINGING FROM THE LEFT
AGAINST THE DLC WING OF THE PARTY,
REPRESENTED BY PRESUMED FRONT-
RUNNER JOHN KERRY. A FORMER DOCTOR,
DEAN PROPOSED UNIVERSAL HEALTH
CARE. HE WANTED TO CAP STUDENT
LOAN DEBT AT $10,000. PRESAGING
DONALD TRUMP, HE PROMISED TO
RENEGOTIATE NAFTA. HE WAS AGAINST
THE IRAQ WAR, THOUGH HE DID SUPPORT
THE OCCUPATION OF AFGHANISTAN.

**How the Internet Invented
Howard Dean**

Forget fundraising (though his opponents sure can't). The real
reason the Doctor is in: He listens to the **Dean nets**
people who use it.

quarter

*The Nation; Howard Dean's
Internet Push: Where Will it Lead?*

DEAN WAS AHEAD OF HIS TIME. MOST
PRESIDENTIAL CAMPAIGNS HIT UP
WEALTHY DONORS FOR CASH.

HE SOLICITED SMALL DONATIONS OVER
THE INTERNET INSTEAD: HIS AVERAGE
DONATION WAS JUST UNDER $80. RAISING
MONEY ONLINE WAS CHEAPER THAN
HOSTING EVENTS OR RUNNING
TELEMARKETING AND DIRECT MAIL
CAMPAIGNS. BECAUSE HIS DONATIONS
WERE MUCH LOWER THAN THE MAXIMUM
ALLOWED BY LAW, HE COULD ASK
SUPPORTERS TO DOUBLE DOWN WHEN HE
FELL SHORT. HE FAVORED A 50-STATE
CAMPAIGN STRATEGY THAT RECOGNIZED
THE POWER OF TELEVISION AND THE
INTERNET TO PUBLICIZE APPEARANCES
BEYOND KEY SWING DISTRICTS.

IF ELECTED, DEAN WOULDN'T BE BEHOLDEN TO CORPORATE INTERESTS. BERNIE SANDERS FOLLOWED THIS TEMPLATE 12 YEARS LATER. DEAN HAD FIGURED OUT CAMPAIGN FINANCING.

HE COLLECTED AN IMPRESSIVE LIST OF ENDORSEMENTS, INCLUDING ONE FROM AL GORE. BUT HE FAILED TO SEDUCE THE CORPORATE MEDIA.

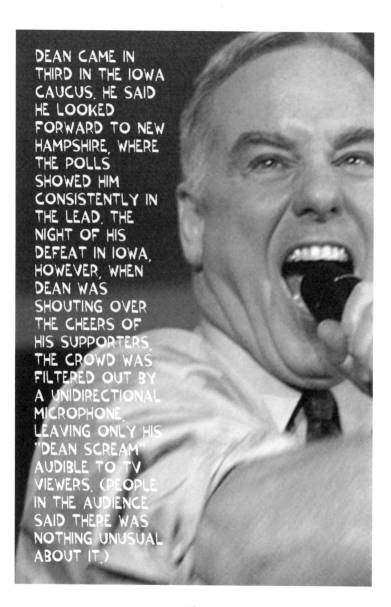

DEAN CAME IN
THIRD IN THE IOWA
CAUCUS. HE SAID
HE LOOKED
FORWARD TO NEW
HAMPSHIRE, WHERE
THE POLLS
SHOWED HIM
CONSISTENTLY IN
THE LEAD. THE
NIGHT OF HIS
DEFEAT IN IOWA,
HOWEVER, WHEN
DEAN WAS
SHOUTING OVER
THE CHEERS OF
HIS SUPPORTERS,
THE CROWD WAS
FILTERED OUT BY
A UNIDIRECTIONAL
MICROPHONE,
LEAVING ONLY HIS
"DEAN SCREAM"
AUDIBLE TO TV
VIEWERS. (PEOPLE
IN THE AUDIENCE
SAID THERE WAS
NOTHING UNUSUAL
ABOUT IT.)

CORPORATE MEDIA OUTLETS, NO DOUBT MORE PUT OFF BY DEAN'S LEFTIE POLITICS THAN HIS "SCREAM," AIRED THE INCIDENT AN ESTIMATED 633 TIMES ON CABLE AND BROADCAST NEWS IN THE FOUR DAYS FOLLOWING THE RALLY. THEIR MESSAGE WAS CLEAR: DEAN WAS UNHINGED.

The Rise And Fall Of Howard Dean

The rise and fall of Howard Dean

An object lesson in Democratic Party politics

What Happened to Howard Dean?

The Front-Runner's Fall

The Dean implosion up close, from the vantage point of the candidate'

HE SANK IN THE POLLS AND SOON DROPPED OUT OF THE RACE, EVENTUALLY REEMERGING AS A COOKIE-CUTTER MSNBC NEWS ANALYST.

THE NOMINATION WENT TO JOHN KERRY, AN ESTABLISHMENT CANDIDATE WHOSE FIREBRAND ACTIVIST DAYS WERE TUCKED FAR IN THE LONG AGO—AND WHO ULTIMATELY FAILED TO STOP GEORGE W. BUSH FROM WINNING A SECOND TERM.

LIKE CHARLIE BROWN REPEATEDLY TRYING TO KICK THE FOOTBALL ONLY TO HAVE LUCY PULL IT AWAY, PROGRESSIVES KEPT TAKING SHOTS AT THE DEMOCRATIC PRESIDENTIAL NOMINATION. MYRIAD WERE THE WAYS THAT WERE FOUND TO STOP THEM IN THEIR TRACKS.

APOLOGIES + APPRECIATION TO SCHULZ

A SUCCESSFUL TRIAL LAWYER FROM
NORTH CAROLINA, JOHN EDWARDS IN
2008 HAD EVERYTHING YOU MIGHT HOPE
FOR WHEN RUNNING FOR THE DEMOCRATIC
PRESIDENTIAL NOMINATION: GOOD LOOKS,
CHARM, INTELLIGENCE, DEEP POCKETS,
AND THE UNIQUE COMBINATION OF
COMING FROM NORTH CAROLINA AND
ESPOUSING A POPULIST APPROACH TO
PROGRESSIVISM THAT COULD UNITE THE
DISPARATE WINGS OF THE PARTY.

I WAS ARROGANT AND DUMB AND DISHONEST AND RECKLESS BUT MOSTLY HORNY.

YOU *EXPECT* SCUMBAGGERY FROM REPUBLICANS.

HOW COULD JOHN EDWARDS BE SO RECKLESS AND HORNY?

LIKE THE OTHER MAJOR CANDIDATE IN THE RACE, NEW YORK SENATOR HILLARY CLINTON, EDWARDS WAS BLINDSIDED BY THE SURPRISING RISE OF THE EVENTUAL WINNER, THE "FAUXGRESSIVE" BARACK OBAMA.

ADDRESSING CENTURIES OF SYSTEMIC DISCRIMINATION IS HARD. VOTING FOR ME IS **EASY**!

ME YOU CAN VOTE FOR

AT THE SUGGESTION OF THE DNC, THE MEDIA FRAMED EDWARDS AS A HYPOCRITE FOR LIVING A WEALTHY LIFESTYLE WHILE ESPOUSING PROGRESSIVE ECONOMIC POLICIES.

"It seems today we have two Americas. With two health care systems, one for the privileged, the other rationed by insurance companies. With two public school systems, one for the haves, one for everybody else. Two governments, one for powerful interests and lobbyists, the other for the rest of us. Two tax systems, where the wealthy corporations pay less, working families pay more."

—John Edwards

"Rather than engage his arguments about corporate control over the political system, the media caricatured Edwards for having a large house, a brief stint working for a hedge fund, and his expensive haircuts."
—Peter Hart, FAIR

BUT THE "LIMOUSINE LIBERAL"
CHARACTERIZATION WASN'T NEARLY AS
HARMFUL AS EDWARDS'S INABILITY TO
GET MEDIA COVERAGE.

The corporate media blackout of John Edwards gets worse

Edwards Poverty Campaign Met With Media Blackout

Total Mentions on Nightly Network News

12/26/07–2/5/08—

- Barack Obama: 1,204
- Hillary Clinton: 992
- John McCain: 931
- Mitt Romney: 904
- Mike Huckabee: 503
- John Edwards: 392

"The press was really so focused on [Hillary] Clinton and Obama that it was going to be tougher and tougher for us to break through."

—Joe Trippi
   John Edwards's campaign manager

IN 2011 THE SPREAD OF THE OCCUPY WALL STREET MOVEMENT TO ENCAMPMENTS ACROSS THE UNITED STATES REMINDED US THAT LEFT-WING ACTIVISM WAS STILL A FORCE IN AMERICAN POLITICS.

A POPULIST REACTION TO OBAMA'S DECISION TO BAIL OUT WALL STREET RATHER THAN MAIN STREET AFTER THE 2008 GLOBAL ECONOMIC CRISIS, THE OCCUPY MOVEMENT LASTED ABOUT THREE GLORIOUS MONTHS AND THEN WAS BRUTALLY CRUSHED IN VIOLENT RAIDS COORDINATED BY THE FEDS.

OCCUPY WAS, LIKE MUCH OF THE LEFT, DIVIDED BETWEEN REVOLUTIONARIES WHO WANTED TO OVERTHROW THE SYSTEM AND GET RID OF CAPITALISM, AND REFORMISTS WHO WANTED TO WORK WITHIN THE ELECTORAL POLITICAL SYSTEM AND THE DEMOCRATIC PARTY.

REFORMISTS MENTIONED POLITICIANS
THEY THOUGHT THEY COULD TRUST:
CONGRESSWOMAN ELIZABETH WARREN,
RESPONSIBLE FOR THE CREATION OF THE
CONSUMER FINANCIAL PROTECTION
BUREAU UNDER OBAMA, AND VERMONT
SENATOR BERNIE SANDERS, THE
INDEPENDENT DEMOCRATIC SOCIALIST.

DURING THE 2008 CAMPAIGN OBAMA HAD CLEVERLY MIXED HIS CORPORATE-FRIENDLY POLICIES WITH ANODYNE RHETORIC THAT SOUNDED VAGUELY PROGRESSIVE.

BY 2011, HOWEVER, ADHERENTS OF THE OCCUPY MOVEMENT WERE HARDLY THE ONLY AMERICANS WHO NOTICED THE PRESIDENT'S INDIFFERENCE TO THE MILLIONS OF AMERICANS STILL OUT OF WORK AND/OR HOMELESS. EVEN THE PRESIDENT'S SIGNATURE ACCOMPLISHMENT, THE AFFORDABLE CARE ACT, FELL SHORT OF HIS OWN PROMISE TO OFFER A SINGLE-PAYER "PUBLIC OPTION" FOR HEALTH INSURANCE.

UNEMPLOYMENT REMAINED HIGH. OBAMA FACED LOW JOB APPROVAL RATINGS. YET NO BOLDFACE-NAME POLITICIAN WAS WILLING TO CONFRONT OBAMA IN THE 2012 PRIMARIES. A REAL CHALLENGE WOULD HAVE TO COME FROM THE LEFT—AND HISTORY SHOWED HOW DIFFICULT THE PARTY WOULD MAKE IT FOR ANYONE WHO DARED TRY.

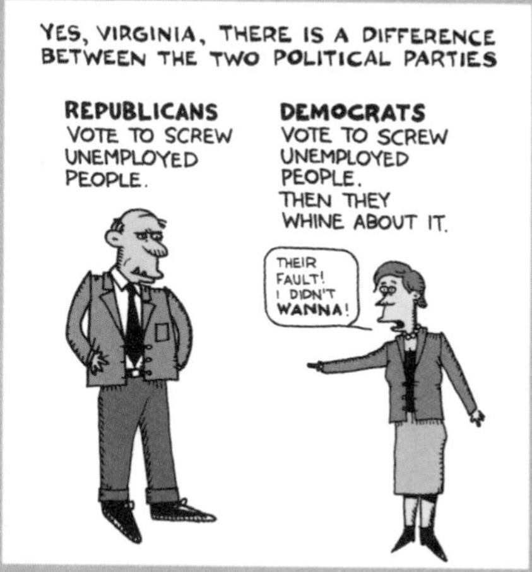
YES, VIRGINIA, THERE IS A DIFFERENCE BETWEEN THE TWO POLITICAL PARTIES
REPUBLICANS VOTE TO SCREW UNEMPLOYED PEOPLE.
DEMOCRATS VOTE TO SCREW UNEMPLOYED PEOPLE. THEN THEY WHINE ABOUT IT.
THEIR FAULT! I DIDN'T WANNA!

DEMOCRATS WHO BOTHERED TO SHOW UP AT THE POLLS THAT SPRING WERE ASKED TO CHOOSE BETWEEN THE INCUMBENT AND SUCH FRINGE FIGURES AS THE ANTI-ABORTION ACTIVIST RANDALL TERRY AND THE PERFORMANCE ARTIST VERMIN SUPREME.

NOT EVERYONE WAS PLEASED ABOUT OBAMA'S CAKEWALK TO THE NOMINATION.

"One of the reasons the president has been able to move so far to the right is that there is no primary opposition to him. And I think it would do this country good if people started thinking about what is a progressive agenda as opposed to what Obama is doing."

—Sanders, 2011

FOUR YEARS LATER, SANDERS WENT AFTER OBAMA'S HANDPICKED IDEOLOGICAL SUCCESSOR ON THE DEMOCRATIC PARTY'S RIGHT FLANK, HILLARY CLINTON.

WHEN I SAT DOWN FOR AN INTERVIEW WITH SANDERS AT JOURNALIST BILL PRESS'S TOWNHOUSE IN WASHINGTON AS PART OF THE RESEARCH FOR MY GRAPHIC BIOGRAPHY, *BERNIE*, HE WAS AT SINGLE DIGITS IN THE POLLS. AT THAT POINT, NO ONE THOUGHT—HIM INCLUDED—THAT HE STOOD A CHANCE.

HE JUST WANTED TO PRESSURE HILLARY TO MOVE TO THE LEFT. IF DONALD TRUMP WAS A DOG CHASING A CAR WHO ACTUALLY CAUGHT ONE, BERNIE SANDERS ALMOST NABBED ONE IN THE FORM OF THE DEMOCRATIC NOMINATION.

WHAT BLOCKED HIM WAS THE DNC.

WIKILEAKS' PUBLICATION OF INTERNAL DNC EMAILS FORCED THE RESIGNATION OF CHAIRMAN DEBBIE WASSERMAN SCHULTZ. DONNA BRAZILE TOOK OVER.

SHE INVESTIGATED BERNIE SANDERS'S ALLEGATION THAT THE PRIMARIES HAD BEEN RIGGED. THE ANSWER, SHE DETERMINED, WAS YES. THE DNC HAD HAD NO CHOICE BUT TO DO CLINTON'S BIDDING.

"Hillary for America (the campaign) and the Hillary Victory Fund (its joint fundraising vehicle with the DNC) had taken care of 80% of the remaining debt in 2016, about $10 million, and had placed the party on an allowance."
—*Newsweek*, 2017

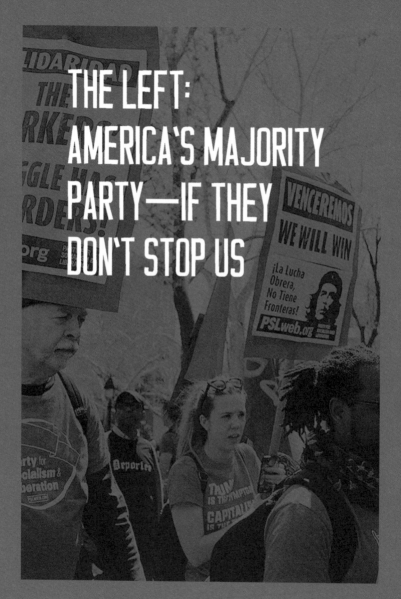

THE LEFT: AMERICA'S MAJORITY PARTY—IF THEY DON'T STOP US

37% OF AMERICANS SELF-IDENTIFY AS SOCIALISTS OR COMMUNISTS.

THAT'S MORE PEOPLE THAN VOTED FOR EITHER HILLARY CLINTON (28% OF ELIGIBLE VOTERS) OR DONALD TRUMP (27%) IN 2016.

IF AMERICA WERE A REAL DEMOCRACY, 37% OF THE VOTERS WOULD HAVE SOMEONE TO VOTE FOR—A CANDIDATE WHO ESPOUSES BELIEFS IN LINE WITH THEIRS.

BUT AMERICA IS NOT REALLY A DEMOCRACY—AND THE DNC IS DETERMINED TO KEEP IT THAT WAY.

Four in 10 Americans prefer socialism to capitalism, poll finds

Reasons for not voting in 2008 election

Too busy
Illness or disability
Not interested / Did not like candidates
Out of town
Registration problems
Transport problems poling place
Forgot
Other reason
Refused

Democrats More Positive About Socialism Than Capitalism

Americans warming to socialism over capitalism, polls show

Biden dings Sanders as a socialist

THOSE WHO WISH TO CREATE A VIABLE POLITICAL PARTY THAT WILL OPPOSE THE CURRENT SYSTEM OF GANGSTER CAPITALISM ARE EXCLUDED FROM DEBATES AND OTHER MEDIA COVERAGE, DENIED BY BALLOT ACCESS RULES THAT THE TWO MAJOR PARTIES CONTROL, AND MALIGNED IN "EDUCATIONAL" PROPAGANDA THAT HAMMERS HOME THE IDEA THAT OUR PRESENT SYSTEM IS THE ONLY ONE WORTH VOTING FOR.

UNSURPRISINGLY, MANY LEFTISTS CHOOSE
NOT TO VOTE RATHER THAN PROP UP A
PARTY THEY SEE AS DEEPLY FLAWED.

VOTER TURNOUT IN TWO-PARTY SYSTEMS
LIKE OURS IS LOWER THAN IN COUNTRIES
LIKE FRANCE, WHICH HAS NUMEROUS PARTIES
ON ITS BALLOTS INCLUDING SEVERAL THAT
ARE UNABASHEDLY MARXIST.

OTHER DISENFRANCHISED LEFTISTS TAKE ON THE TWO-PARTY TRAP, TRYING TO TAKE OVER THE DEMOCRATIC PARTY FROM INSIDE.

A LONG-MARGINALIZED FIGURE WHO REMAINS AN INDEPENDENT EVEN WHEN RUNNING FOR THE DEMOCRATIC PARTY NOMINATION, BERNIE SANDERS HAS COME CLOSER THAN ANY OTHER POLITICAL FIGURE IN MEMORY TO FULFILLING THE DREAM OF A PROGRESSIVE DEMOCRATIC PARTY.

THE LEFTIE WHO CAME IN FROM THE COLD

DESPITE FACING NUMEROUS INSTITUTIONAL OBSTACLES SANDERS COMES SHOCKINGLY CLOSE TO CAPTURING THE 2016 NOMINATION.

DESPITE THEIR CLOSE CALL NEITHER CLINTON NOR THE PARTY LEADERSHIP ACCEPT THE FACT THAT PROGRESSIVES ARE NO LONGER A TINY MINORITY THAT CAN BE TAKEN FOR GRANTED BUT A POTENT FORCE, A MAJORITY WITHIN THE DEMOCRATS AND A PLURALITY OVERALL, ONE THAT WILL MAKE OR BREAK NOMINEES.

CORPORATE MODERATES STILL DON'T GET IT. WHICH IS WHY THE PARTY CHAIRMAN IS TOM PEREZ, A HILLARY CLINTON ALLY. PROGRESSIVES ARE NOW THE PARTY BASE, PRESIDED OVER BY CENTRIST BOSSES THEY LOATHE.

THE DNC MARKETS ITSELF AS THE LEADERSHIP OF THE PARTY OF THE COMMON MAN AND WOMAN, BUT IT HASN'T BEEN ABLE TO DELIVER CLASS-BASED REFORMS AND POLICIES THAT WOULD ACTUALLY SUPPORT THOSE PEOPLE WHEN THEY ARE IN NEED OF HELP.

THE DNC HAS EMBRACED A BRAND OF IDENTITY POLITICS DEVOID OF CLASS CONSCIOUSNESS BECAUSE THEY LIKE THE SYSTEM THE WAY IT IS, LIP SERVICE WITH-OUT SOUND POLICIES TO MAKE THEM ACTUALLY MEAN SOMETHING IMPORTANT.

THE DEMOCRATIC PARTY TODAY IS LESS
ABOUT HISTORICALLY DISADVANTAGED
GROUPS LIKE ETHNIC MINORITIES AND
WOMEN THAN IT IS ABOUT URBAN,
UPWARDLY MOBILE MINORITIES AND
WOMEN.

SO WHEN DONALD TRUMP TARGETS
NAFTA AND OTHER TRADE POLICIES
PUSHED THROUGH BY DEMOCRATS THAT
GUTTED THE INDUSTRIAL MIDWEST AND
THE WHITE WORKING CLASS, THOSE
INTERNAL CONTRADICTIONS WITHIN THE
DEMOCRATIC PARTY ARE EXPOSED.

THE CRISIS HAS CREATED OPPORTUNITY
FOR PROGRESSIVES TO TAKE BACK A
PARTY THAT HAS NOT REALLY BEEN
OURS SINCE THE 1960s.

THE 2020 PRIMARY CAMPAIGN HAS SHOWN THAT AT LEAST SOME PARTY LEADERS UNDERSTAND THAT THEY NEED TO TURN OVER THE REINS TO THE LEFT.

NEARLY ALL THE MAJOR DEMOCRATIC CANDIDATES ADOPTED BERNIE SANDERS'S CHIEF LEFT-POPULIST POLICIES: A $15-AN-HOUR MINIMUM WAGE, FREE PUBLIC COLLEGE, AND MEDICARE FOR ALL. ALEXANDRIA OCASIO-CORTEZ'S "GREEN NEW DEAL" WAS EMBRACED BY MUCH OF THE FIELD AS WELL.

CALIFORNIA SENATOR KAMALA HARRIS, A HARD-AS-NAILS FORMER PROSECUTOR WHO SENT AN INNOCENT MAN TO DEATH ROW, POINTEDLY DENIED BEING A "DEMOCRATIC SOCIALIST."

BUT SHE KNEW SHE HAD TO PAY LIP SERVICE TO PROGRESSIVISM. SHE ENDORSED ALL THREE OF SANDERS'S PLANKS, THOUGH SHE INSISTED MEDICARE FOR ALL ISN'T SOCIALIST.

FINALLY SHE ABANDONED THE RACE, AT LEAST IN PART BECAUSE HER POSITIONS SEEMED TOO WISHY-WASHY. SENATORS CORY BOOKER, KIRSTEN GILLIBRAND, AND ELIZABETH WARREN, A FORMER REPUBLICAN, ALL ENDORSED THE PROGRESSIVE POLICY TRINITY.

STILL, THE RIGHT-WING DREAMS OF THE
RULING ELITES REFUSE TO DIE.

JOE BIDEN, THE 78-YEAR-OLD FORMER
VICE PRESIDENT, APPEARS TO BE
SUFFERING FROM EARLY SIGNS OF
DEMENTIA. BUT THIS DIDN'T STOP PARTY
LEADERS FROM REQUISITIONING HIM TO
ENTER THE RACE AT THE LAST MOMENT.

HE DOESN'T HAVE MUCH OF AN AGENDA
BUT HIS PURPOSE IN THE RACE IS CLEAR:
PRESENT A MODERATE AGENDA TO
PREVENT PROGRESSIVE ELIZABETH WARREN
OR PROGRESSIVE BERNIE SANDERS FROM
BECOMING PRESIDENT.

AFTER HIS BEFUDDLEMENT AND POLICY MODERATION CAUSED BIDEN'S CAMPAIGN TO LAG, WORRIED PARTY DONORS AND CLINTONITE DNC LEADERS ENCOURAGED MICHAEL BLOOMBERG, FORMER NEW YORK CITY MAYOR, REAL ESTATE BILLIONAIRE, FORMER REPUBLICAN, AND MEDIA TYCOON FAR TO THE RIGHT OF THE PARTY, TO "RESCUE" THE PARTY FROM SANDERS AND WARREN, WHO TOGETHER WERE POLLING AT ABOUT HALF OF PRIMARY VOTERS.

BEFORE LONG ALL THE CANDIDATES BUT WARREN HAD FALLEN IN LINE BEHIND BIDEN. IT WAS A TWO-MAN RACE: BIDEN VS. SANDERS, MODERATE VS. PROGRESSIVE.

WHAT'S LEFT

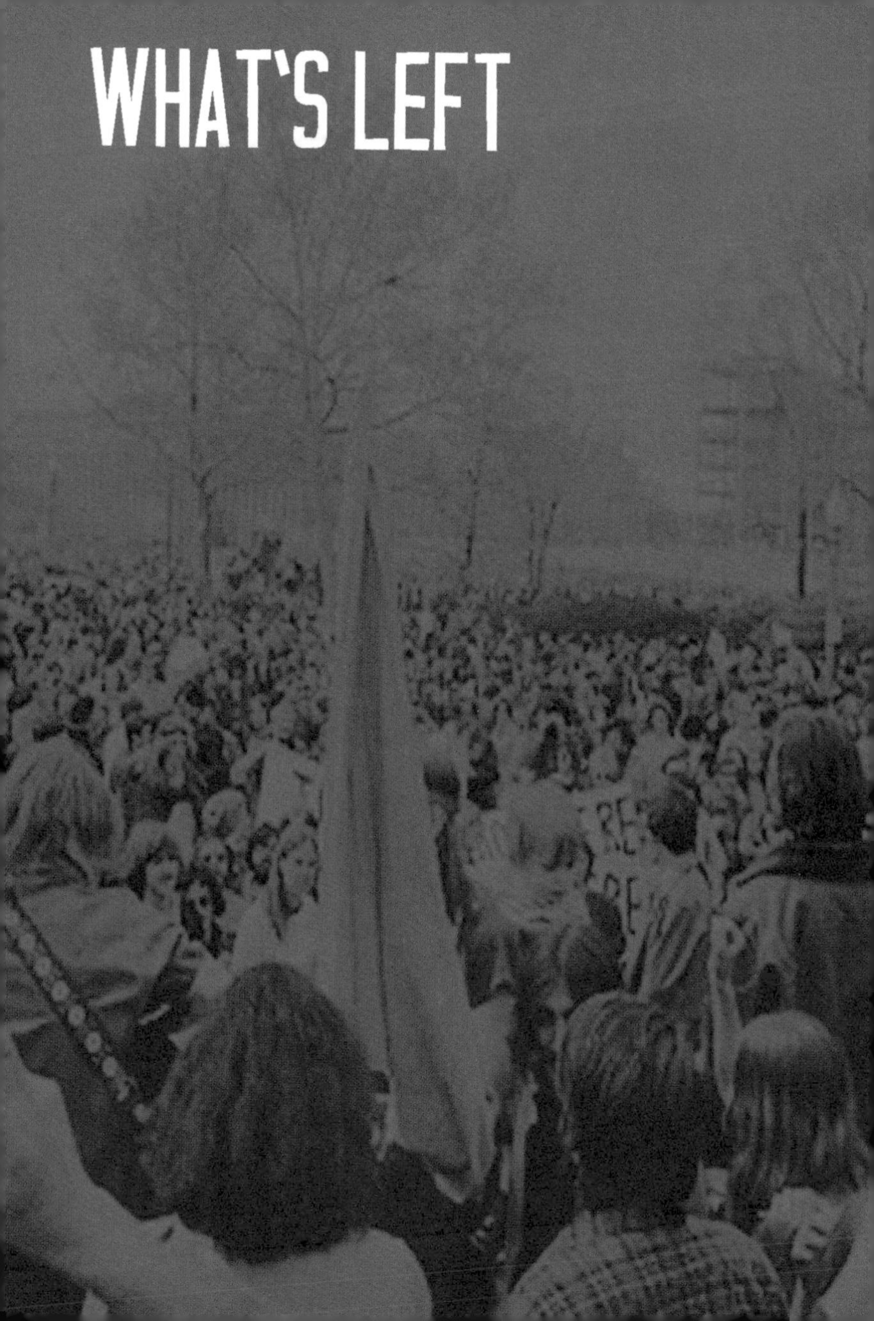

SO WHAT DOES IT MEAN TO BE PROGRESSIVE?

MORE THAN A 2020 PASTICHE OF A 19th-CENTURY POPULAR TRADITION, TODAY PROGRESSIVISM STANDS FOR ANTI-CORPORATISM, ANTI-GLOBALISM, ENVIRONMENTALISM, AND COMMON DECENCY WHEN IT COMES TO SOCIAL POLICY. A REACTION TO THE EXCESSES OF THE LAST HALF-CENTURY, IT BOILS DOWN TO THE SLOGAN "PEOPLE BEFORE PROFITS."

FOR PROGRESSIVES, WORKING PEOPLE ARE WHAT MAKE AMERICA GREAT AND STRONG. WORKERS DESERVE A BIGGER SHARE OF THE GOOD THINGS THAT RESULT FROM THEIR LABOR.

SO A HIGH MINIMUM WAGE IS ESSENTIAL.

UPPER-MIDDLE-CLASS PEOPLE DON'T EAT HERE CUZ SEEING YOUR MISERABLE FACES MAKES THEM FEEL DIRTY. SO YOU'RE GETTING A RAISE.

A **TINY** RAISE.

AND IT'S NOT FOR YOU. ONLY 10% OF THE RESTAURANTS ARE COMPANY-OWNED. THIS IS A FRANCHISE.

BACK TO WORK.

WHY DO THE **RICH GET RICHER** AND THE **POOR GET POORER**? BECAUSE CAPITALISM ENCOURAGES **MONOPOLIES** AND CONCENTRATES WEALTH INTO FEWER HANDS.

INEQUALITY ISN'T A FLAW. IT'S A **FEATURE**. THE EXISTENCE OF POVERTY TERRORIZES WORKERS INTO ACCEPTING LOW WAGES AND MOTIVATES THEM TO STRIVE HARD.

I MADE MY MONEY THE OLD-FASHIONED WAY: WE BOUGHT OUR SMARTEST COMPETITORS AND SHUT THEM DOWN.

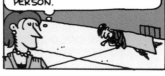

THERE BUT FOR THE GRACE OF— EXCEPT, **I'M** A GOOD PERSON.

PROGRESSIVES ARE DETERMINED TO REVERSE THE DECADES-LONG TREND OF INCREASING INCOME INEQUALITY AND WEALTH ACCUMULATION. AMERICA'S BIFURCATED ECONOMY IS INTRINSICALLY UNFAIR AND INCOMPATIBLE WITH THE DECLARATION OF INDEPENDENCE AND ITS PROMISE THAT EVERYONE OUGHT TO BE EMPOWERED TO PURSUE HAPPINESS.

FEW PROGRESSIVES ARE COMMUNISTS: THEY DON'T WANT A STATE ECONOMY. BUT MOST ARE SOCIALIST OR DEMOCRATIC SOCIALIST, THE SCANDINAVIAN ECONOMIC MODEL TOUTED BY SANDERS.

PROGRESSIVES WANT POLITICIAN-
REPRESENTATIVES INDEPENDENT OF
MONIED INTERESTS.

ELECTED OFFICIALS SHOULD NOT ACCEPT
CORPORATE CONTRIBUTIONS.

CAPITALISM SHOULD BE HIGHLY REGULATED AND CONTROLLED TO MAKE SURE THAT COMPANIES DON'T POLLUTE OR OTHERWISE ENDANGER PUBLIC HEALTH.

GOVERNMENT MUST SMASH MONOPOLIES AND ENSURE THAT A SIGNIFICANT SHARE OF PROFITS RESULTING FROM PRODUCTIVITY IS RETURNED TO WORKERS AND, VIA CORPORATE TAXES TO PAY FOR GOVERNMENT SERVICES SUCH AS HEALTH CARE AND TRANSPORTATION, TO THE CITIZENRY.

THE SOCIAL SAFETY NET MUST BE WIDE AND THICK, ENCOMPASSING ALL THE NECESSITIES OF LIFE: FOOD, SHELTER, EDUCATION, TRANSPORTATION, AND HEALTH CARE.

IF A CITIZEN FALLS DOWN, THE GOVERNMENT SHOULD HELP HIM OR HER GET BACK UP. PROGRESSIVES WANT TO SEE OLD-FASHIONED ANTI-POVERTY PROGRAMS, WELL-FUNDED ONES. THEY WANT GOVERNMENT ASSISTANCE TO INCLUDE THE WORKING POOR AND LOWER MIDDLE CLASS, NOT JUST THE INDIGENT.

156

PRICE GOUGING, PROFITEERING, AND HUGE EXECUTIVE SALARIES SHOULD BE PROHIBITED BY LAW.

THE CEOs OF BIG RETAILERS AND RESTAURANTS LIKE WAL-MART, MACY'S, WENDY'S AND STARBUCKS "EARN" $5,859/HOUR.   — USA TODAY

PRIVACY RIGHTS MUST BE RESPECTED.
ORWELLIAN SURVEILLANCE SCHEMES LIKE
FACIAL RECOGNITION SOFTWARE USED IN
PUBLIC SPACES, SURVEILLANCE CAMERAS,
AND NATIONAL SECURITY AGENCY SPYING
ON AMERICAN CITIZENS ARE ANATHEMA.

SILICON VALLEY TECH FIRMS LIKE SOCIAL
MEDIA COMPANIES SHOULD BE PROHIBITED
FROM TURNING OUR PRIVATE
INFORMATION INTO THEIR PRODUCT.

THE ENVIRONMENT MUST BE PRIORITIZED OVER CORPORATE PROFITS.

PROGRESSIVES BELIEVE THAT THE CLIMATE CHANGE CRISIS IS THE MOST PRESSING ISSUE OF ALL.

PROGRESSIVES ARE SKEPTICAL OF IDENTITY POLITICS-BASED POLICIES LIKE AFFIRMATIVE ACTION BUT ACCEPT THEM IF THEY ARE BASED ON CLASS AS WELL AS ETHNICITY.

WE ABSOLUTELY BELIEVE IN EQUALITY BASED ON RACE, GENDER, SEXUAL ORIENTATION, ETC., AND SUPPORT LEGISLATION TO CREATE A MORE EQUAL SOCIETY.

MOST PROGRESSIVES ARE OPPOSED TO MILITARISM AND ESPECIALLY TO FOREIGN ADVENTURISM.

IMAGINE...

FIRST WE'D LIKE TO INVITE WORKERS IN HELPING PROFESSIONS TO PRE-BOARD: TEACHERS, NURSES, SOCIAL WORKERS, THOSE IN CHARITIES. NEXT WILL BE PEACE ACTIVISTS, UNION REPS, AND JOURNALISTS. THEN WE'LL BOARD BY ROW, WITH RICH PIGS LAST.

WE WOULD CUT BACK DEFENSE SPENDING, BRING HOME AMERICAN TROOPS FROM FOREIGN ENTANGLEMENTS, AND CLOSE MOST OF THE OVER-1,000 MILITARY BASES AROUND THE WORLD.

AN EXCEPTION WOULD BE LIMITED HUMANITARIAN MISSIONS LIKE STOPPING THE GENOCIDE IN BOSNIA, FOLLOWED BY A RAPID WITHDRAWAL.

IF DEMOCRATS ARE TO DEFEAT REPUBLICANS—WHICH, CONSIDERING THAT WE HAVE MORE REGISTERED VOTERS, SHOULD BE THE RULE, NOT THE EXCEPTION—THE CENTRISTS STILL RUNNING THE DNC NEED TO STEP ASIDE AND SHARE POWER AT THE TOP OF THE PARTY LEADERSHIP WITH THE NEW PROGRESSIVE WING.

CENTRISTS NEED PROGRESSIVE VOICES MORE THAN PROGRESSIVES NEED CENTRISTS. GIVEN THE GRIM HISTORICAL RECORD OF INTERNECINE WARFARE WITHIN THE DEMOCRATIC PARTY AT THE HANDS OF THE DLC AND DNC, IS THERE EVEN A FUTURE FOR A PROGRESSIVE-CENTRIST ALLIANCE WITHIN THE DEMOCRATIC PARTY?

IT'S UP TO THE CENTRISTS NOW TO SHOW THEIR GOOD FAITH.

IF SO, PROGRESSIVES WILL BE INVITED TO BECOME FULL PARTNERS IN DEMOCRATIC PARTY LEADERSHIP IN TERMS OF STRATEGY, TACTICS, PLATFORM PLANKS, ETC., AND WE WILL SEE A REINVIGORATED BASE TURN OUT THE VOTE AS NEVER BEFORE AND WIN ELECTION AFTER ELECTION ON BEHALF OF SOCIAL JUSTICE AND THE PURSUIT OF HAPPINESS FOR THE MAJORITY OF THE PEOPLE.

...AS OPPOSED TO THE EXISTING SITUATION, SOMEWHAT ANALOGOUS TO APARTHEID SOUTH AFRICA, WHERE A TINY MINORITY CONTROLLED THE VAST MAJORITY. A 72% PROGRESSIVE PARTY BASE CANNOT BE LED SUCCESSFULLY BY CENTRIST LEADERSHIP.

IF THE DEMOCRATIC PARTY IS TO REMAIN VIABLE—AND THERE'S A STRONG ARGUMENT THAT SAYS IT SHOULD NOT AND CANNOT—THE CENTRIST LEADERSHIP IS GOING TO HAVE TO YIELD, AND DO SO SOON.

HOW DOES ONE RECONCILE CENTRISM
THAT SUCKS UP TO CORPORATIONS AND
HAS FULLY EMBRACED AGGRESSIVE
MILITARISM WITH PROGRESSIVISM, WHICH IS
VIOLENTLY OPPOSED TO THOSE THINGS?

IT MAY NOT BE POSSIBLE.

ENVIRONMENT:

SAVE ½ THE PLANET!

HEALTH CARE:

SAVE ½ THE PEOPLE!

MILITARY:

½ AS MANY WAR CRIMES!

GENERAL ELECTION:

½ AS MANY VOTES!

IT WOULD BE NICE TO THINK THAT
CENTRISTS WOULD BE ABLE TO COPY
BERNIE SANDERS'S SMALL-DONATION
MODEL IN ORDER TO FREE THEMSELVES
OF DEPENDENCY ON WALL STREET
MONEY.

BUT BARACK OBAMA DID THAT IN 2008
AND SOLD OUT ANYWAY. PERHAPS IT
WASN'T REALLY SELLING OUT.
CORPORATE DEMOCRATS MIGHT
ACTUALLY BELIEVE THAT PROFITS HAVE
TO COME BEFORE PEOPLE, IN PURE
CAPITALISM IN OTHER WORDS.

THE DYING GASPS OF THE DEMOCRATS'
AGING PRO-CORPORATE LEADERSHIP MAKE
CLEAR THAT THE STRUGGLE WITHIN THE
PARTY CONTINUES.

WILL WE ELECT BERNIE SANDERS, OR
SOMEONE LIKE HIM? AND IF NOT, WHY
NOT? CLEARLY, MOST AMERICANS WANT
TO LIVE IN A SOCIETY WHERE HEALTH
CARE AND A UNIVERSITY EDUCATION ARE
ESSENTIALLY THINGS THAT EVERY
AMERICAN IS ENTITLED TO.

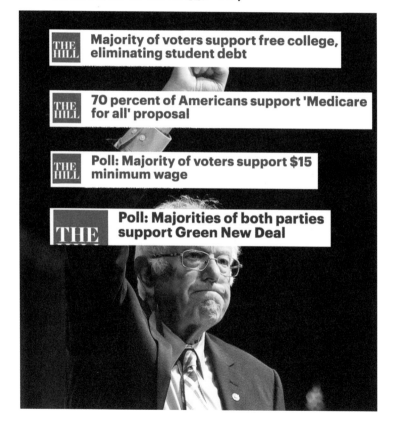

THE HILL Majority of voters support free college, eliminating student debt

THE HILL 70 percent of Americans support 'Medicare for all' proposal

THE HILL Poll: Majority of voters support $15 minimum wage

THE Poll: Majorities of both parties support Green New Deal

WHEN THE CORONAVIRUS ARRIVED FROM CHINA AND COMPLETELY UPENDED THE U.S. ECONOMY AND EVERYDAY LIFE, THE NEED FOR HEALTH CARE AS A BASIC HUMAN RIGHT—FOR WHICH SANDERS HAD BEEN FIGHTING—BECAME ABUNDANTLY CLEAR TO EVERYONE.

FOR PEOPLE WHO SAY MEDICARE FOR ALL IS NOT REALISTIC, WHAT DO THEY STAND FOR? THE RIGHTS OF GIANT CORPORATIONS LIKE GOOGLE AND FACEBOOK TO MINT BILLIONAIRES AND USE OUR PRIVATE INFORMATION AS THEIR MAIN PRODUCT?

IF CORPORATE DEMOCRATS GET THEIR WAY, THE DEMOCRATIC PARTY WILL CONTINUE TO BE THE PLACE WHERE LEFTIST MOVEMENTS GO TO DIE. YOU CAN EVEN SEE IT IN THEIR IMPEACHMENT INQUIRY INTO DONALD TRUMP, WHICH FOCUSED ON HIS FAILED ATTEMPTS AT CORRUPT DEALS IN UKRAINE BUT LARGELY IGNORED HIS COUNTLESS SUCCESSFUL CORRUPT DEALINGS RIGHT HERE AT HOME.

IT MAY NOT HAVE BEEN INTENTIONAL, BUT THE PRACTICAL EFFECT OF IMPEACHMENT WAS TO DISTRACT THE COUNTRY FROM ITS FIRST-EVER NATIONAL DIALOGUE ABOUT POLICY PROPOSALS THAT WOULD REALLY HELP PEOPLE, LIKE MEDICARE FOR ALL. IT EVEN STIFLED DEBATE ABOUT THE GREEN NEW DEAL, WHICH MAY BE OUR LAST CHANCE TO STOP USING GREENHOUSE-GAS-PRODUCING FOSSIL FUELS.

THE FIGHT FOR THE SOUL OF THE
DEMOCRATIC PARTY MAY WELL WIND UP
DETERMINING THE FATE OF HUMANKIND.

WHAT HAPPENS NEXT?

IT'S SIMPLE.

PROGRESSIVES WILL TAKE OVER THE
DEMOCRATIC PARTY AND CHANGE
AMERICAN POLITICS FOREVER.

OR THE CENTRISTS WILL KEEP THEIR PARTY.

We attended professional sporting events 158 million times a year.

We organized to overthrow the system that is burning up the earth, to save ourselves, 0 minutes.

AND IF PROGRESSIVES GIVE UP ON THE
DEMOCRATS? THEY'LL EITHER WALLOW IN
APATHY AND ALIENATION, OR THEY'LL
FIND ANOTHER WAY TO TRY TO BRING
AMERICA TO ITS SENSES.

A NEW PARTY?

The Democrats'll get in.

If they want, they'll repeal all of Trump's Republican crap.

If they want.

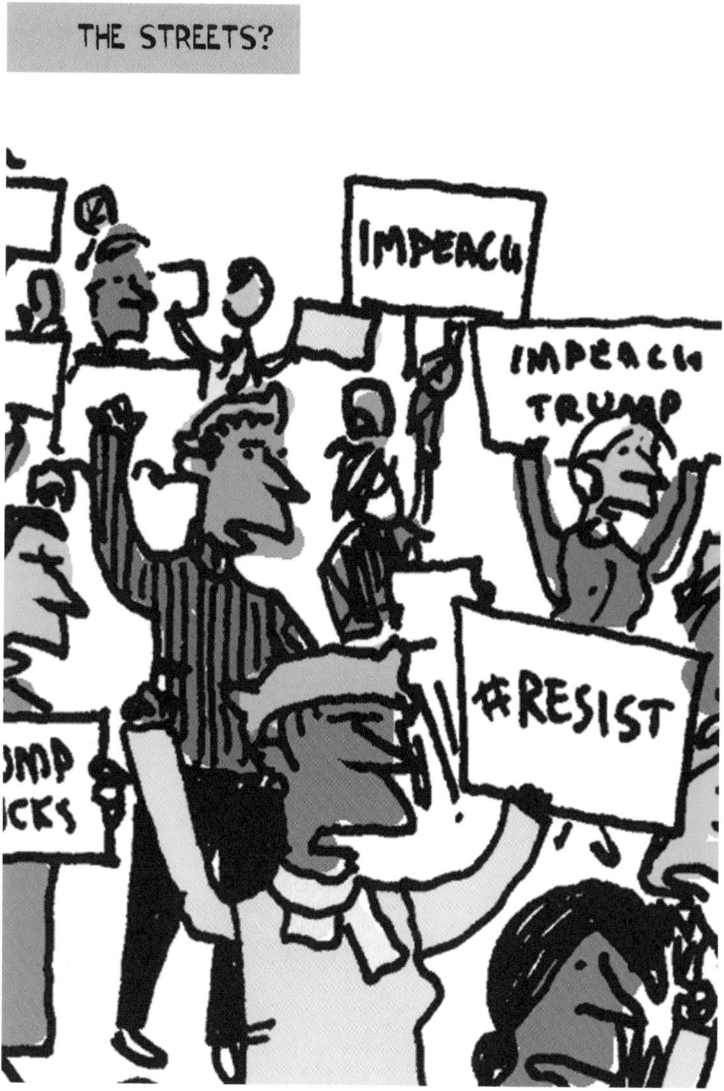
THE STREETS?
IMPEACH
IMPEACH TRUMP
#RESIST

OR SOMETHING ELSE?

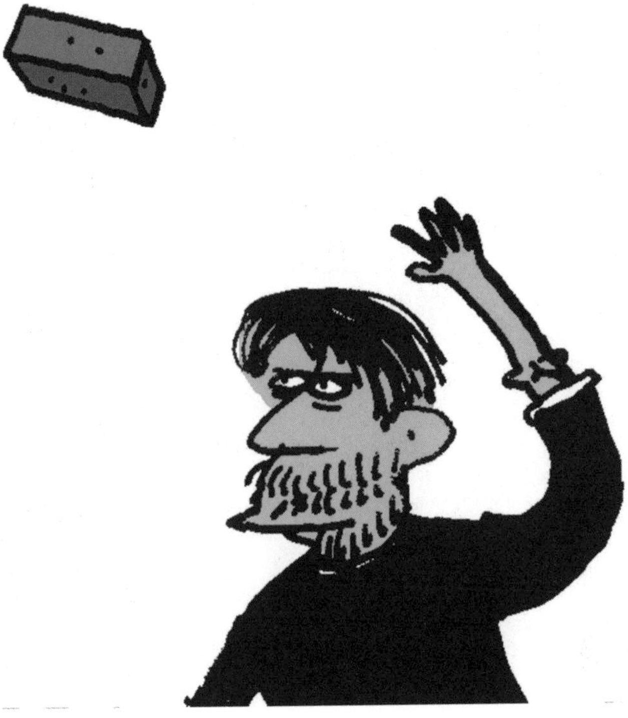

THE PAST IS PROLOGUE. BUT AS JOE STRUMMER SAID, THE FUTURE IS UNWRITTEN.

Afterword

Can the Civil War in the Democratic Party be resolved? Ultimately, I think the answer is no.

Don't get me wrong. There would be a lot to be said for preserving the postwar coalition between the actual left and anti-communist liberals, an alliance now between progressives and neoliberals. That alliance has kept Republicans at bay many times. It has made tremendous social and economic progress, particularly between FDR and LBJ. But I don't think it has much of a future.

The history of the schism between the left and right wing of the Democratic Party is documented in this book, and what it shows is that the right wing controls the party even though the vast majority of Democratic voters are of the left. And that right wing is far more interested in preserving its control of one of the two major parties than it is in defeating the Republicans.

In the end, however, what makes these differences irreconcilable is not attitudinal. It's ideological.

The underlying assumption is that left-wing and right-wing Democrats fall on some sort of ideological continuum. In other words, progressives are simply more pure whereas centrists are more pragmatic. But both of them pretty much want the same things.

That's not true.

Progressives oppose all wars of choice. Moderates are in favor of many wars of choice. There is no middle ground between these two positions. Starting half as many wars would not please progressives enough to keep them in the party.

Progressives want socialized health care; they want doctors and nurses to work for the government. Barack Obama came up with a plan that attempted to strike a middle ground between the progressive position and the "let the free market work its magic" position of Democratic moderates. But the Affordable Care Act ended up pleasing no one. As far as progressives are concerned, it actually made things worse because it created the illusion that the American health care crisis had been resolved by legislation when in fact the underlying problems of high costs and runaway insurance profits continue.

Progressivism and Democratic centrism/moderation are two discrete ideologies, not related but in fact opposed to one another. They can no more be in political partnership than a cat and a mouse.

These two factions, I think, should be two different parties.

The same, by the way, applies to the uneasy pairing of major factions within the Republican Party. The corporate business wing of the party, obsessed with making profits, has little to nothing in common with the Tea Party radicals or, for that matter, Christian evangelicals. These guys don't belong together. They have irreconcilable differences.

What would be wrong with more parties?

More democracy?

Notes

10. No one knows how WikiLeaks received the DNC data dump. U.S. corporate media accepts the intelligence agencies' assessment that the source was the Russian government. Indeed, the DNC appears to have been hacked by Russia. But Craig Murray, former British ambassador to Uzbekistan, a progressive who works with WikiLeaks, says he received it by hand from a disgruntled DNC staffer at a park near American University in Washington. Julian Assange of WikiLeaks confirms that the source was not a state actor, which rules out Russia. Computer experts say the download rate is consistent with connection to a thumb drive as opposed to accessing over the Internet, which seems to corroborate Murray's account that it was a leak rather than a hack. Whatever the source, no one denies that the material is authentic.

Alana Abramson and Shushannah Walshe, "The 4 Most Damaging Emails from the DNC WikiLeaks Dump," ABC News, July 25, 2016, https://abcnews.go.com/Politics/damaging-emails-dnc-wikileaks-dump/story?id=40852448.

12. Abramson and Walshe, "Most Damaging Emails."

15. "Five Leaders in 2016 Republican White House Race, Quinnipiac University National Poll Finds; Rubio, Paul Are Only Republicans Even Close to Clinton," Quinnipiac University Poll, May 28, 2015, https://poll.qu.edu/national/release-detail?ReleaseID=2228.

16. Dan Roberts, "Bernie Sanders Sees Poll Surge After Series of Record-Breaking Appearances," *Guardian*, July 2, 2015, https://www.theguardian.com/us-news/2015/jul/02/bernie-sanders-poll-surge-hillary-clinton.

16. Cameron Easley, "Poll: Sanders Pulls Closer to Clinton than Ever," Morning Consult, April 18, 2016, https://morningconsult.com/2016/04/18/bernie-sanders-hillary-clinton-democratic-presidential-poll/.

17. Scott Detrow, "Clinton Campaign Had Additional Signed Agreement with DNC in 2015," NPR, November 3, 2017, https://www.npr.

org/2017/11/03/561976645/clinton-campaign-had-additional-signed-agreement-with-dnc-in-2015.

17. Hadas Gold, "Saturday Nights with Hillary, Bernie and Martin," *Politico*, November 13, 2015, https://www.politico.com/story/2015/11/democratic-debates-saturdays-215842.

18. Associated Press in Chicago, "Democrats Change Superdelegates Rules that Enraged Sanders Supporters," *Guardian*, August 25, 2018, https://www.theguardian.com/us-news/2018/aug/25/democrats-rules-superdelegates-sanders.

19. Kevin Drum, "Here's the Joint Fundraising Agreement Between Hillary Clinton and the DNC," *Mother Jones*, November 4, 2017, https://www.motherjones.com/kevin-drum/2017/11/heres-the-joint-fundraising-agreement-between-hillary-clinton-and-the-dnc/.

19. Alexandra Wilts, "Democrats Rigged the 2016 Primary for Hillary Clinton, Claims Former DNC Chair," *Independent*, November 2, 2017, https://www.independent.co.uk/news/world/americas/us-politics/donna-brazile-hillary-clinton-dnc-primary-rigged-bernie-sanders-a8034716.html.

20. Michael Sainato, "Wikileaks Proves Primary Was Rigged: DNC Undermined Democracy," *Observer*, July 22, 2016, https://observer.com/2016/07/wikileaks-proves-primary-was-rigged-dnc-undermined-democracy/.

35. "Party Realignment and the New Deal," History, Art and Archives, accessed December 16, 2019, https://history.house.gov/Exhibitions-and-Publications/BAIC/Historical-Essays/Keeping-the-Faith/Party-Realignment--New-Deal/.

37. "Our Documents: Franklin Roosevelt's Address Announcing the Second New Deal, October 31, 1936," Franklin D. Roosevelt Presidential Library and Museum, accessed December 16, 2019, http://docs.fdrlibrary.marist.edu/od2ndst.html.

41. Ruy Teixeira and Alan Abramowitz, "Decline of the White Working Class and the Rise of a Mass Upper Middle Class," Brookings Institution, April 2008, https://www.brookings.edu/wp-content/uploads/2016/06/04_demographics_teixeira.pdf.

46. Teixeira and Abramowitz, "Decline."

54. "Benefits and Penalties," Selective Service System, accessed December 16, 2019, https://www.sss.gov/Registration/Why-Register/Benefits-and-Penalties.

55. Carter accepted the counsel of his hawkish national security adviser Zbigniew Brzezinski to draw the USSR into what he called the "Afghan Trap." The goal was to bog down the Soviets in their own Vietnam-style quagmire in the so-called graveyard of empires. Though Soviet premier Mikhail Gorbachev ultimately admitted defeat and ordered his forces to withdraw from Afghanistan, Brzezinski's strategy left the Soviet military demoralized. The collapse of the Soviet Union in 1991 was caused by a perfect storm of colliding political and economic forces, including this, the after-effects of the Chernobyl disaster, and other factors.

55. Terrence Smith, "Why Carter Admitted the Shah," *New York Times*, May 17, 1981, https://www.nytimes.com/1981/05/17/magazine/why-carter-admitted-the-shah.html.

58. Shifting labels create some confusion. Progressivism, the early 20th-century populist movement championed by Wisconsin's Robert LaFollette and President Theodore Roosevelt, had withered away by FDR's time. Yet the policies of progressivism were championed by self-defined progressives until the 1990s. As liberals turned hawkish and corporate, left-leaning Democrats who sought to distinguish themselves from liberals drew from history to revive the progressive mantle. The current progressive-liberal split fueled the Occupy Wall Street movement of 2011. But things can and will change again.

61. Michael Kelly, "The 1992 Campaign: The Democrats, Clinton Uses Farm Speech to Begin New Offensive," *New York Times*, September 28, 1992, https://www.nytimes.com/1992/09/28/us/the-1992-campaign-the-democrats-clinton-uses-farm-speech-to-begin-new-offensive.html.

62. Carol E. Lee and Jonathan Martin, "Obama: 'I Am a New Democrat,'" *Politico*, March 10, 2009, https://www.politico.com/story/2009/03/obama-i-am-a-new-democrat-019862.

66. Hedrick Smith, "Democrats Back Carter on Nomination Rule; Kennedy Withdraws from Presidential Race," *New York Times*, August 12, 1980, https://archive.nytimes.com/www.nytimes.com/library/politics/camp/80081 2convention-dem-ra.html.

67. Tim Perry, "Political Playback: A Look Back at the 1980 Democratic Convention," CBS News, May 23, 2016, https://www.cbsnews.com/news/political-playback-a-look-back-at-the-1980-democratic-convention.

68. Jon Ward, "The Humiliating Handshake and the Near-Fistfight that Broke the Democratic Party," *Politico*, January 21, 2019, https://www.politico.com/magazine/story/2019/01/21/camelots-end-kennedy-vs-carter-democratic-convention-1980-224030.

76. "The Reagan Revolution," ER Services, accessed December 16, 2019, https://courses.lumenlearning.com/suny-ushistory2os2xmaster/chapter/the-reagan-revolution/.

76. Marjorie Hunter, "Cuts in U.S. Aid to Education to Have Wide Impact; The Budget Targets First of a Series on Key Programs; That President Reagan Wants to Cut," *New York Times*, April 3, 1981, https://www.nytimes.com/1981/04/03/us/cuts-us-aid-education-have-wide-impact-budget-targets-first-series-key-programs.html.

77. Myles Karp, "WTF Happened to Government Cheese?," *Vice*, February 19, 2018, https://www.vice.com/en_us/article/wn7mgq/wtf-happened-to-government-cheese.
    Dr. E. Fuller Torrey, "Ronald Reagan's Shameful Legacy: Violence, the Homeless, Mental Illness," *Salon*, September 29, 2013, https://www.salon.com/2013/09/29/ronald_reagans_shameful_legacy_violence_the_homeless_mental_illness/.

78. Leanna Garfield, "The 11 Biggest Marches and Protests in American History," *Business Insider*, February 8, 2017, https://www.businessinsider.com/largest-marches-us-history-2017-2.

84. Dwyer Gunn, "What Caused the Decline of Unions in America?," *Pacific Standard*, April 24, 2018, https://psmag.com/economics/what-caused-the-decline-of-unions-in-america.

86. David E. Rosenbaum, "Jackson Makes Formal Bid for Presidency in 1988," *New York Times*, October 11, 1987, https://www.nytimes.com/1987/10/11/us/jackson-makes-formal-bid-for-presidency-in-1988.html.

89. Ta-Nehisi Coates, "The Tragedy of Jesse Jackson," *Atlantic*, July 14, 2008, https://www.theatlantic.com/entertainment/archive/2008/07/the-tragedy-of-jesse-jackson/4984/.

97. Harry G. Levine, "Ralph Nader as Mad Bomber," Internet Archive, March 2004, https://web.archive.org/web/20150211121603/http://hereinstead.com/Ralph-Nader-As-Mad-Bomber.html.

99. "Nader Blocked at Debate Door," *New York Times*, October 4, 2000, https://www.nytimes.com/2000/10/04/politics/nader-blocked-at-debate-door.html.

108. Evelyn Nieves, "Conversation/Ralph Nader; A Party Crasher's Lone Regret: That He Didn't Get More Votes," *New York Times*, February 18, 2001, https://www.nytimes.com/2001/02/18/weekinreview/conversation-ralph-nader-party-crasher-s-lone-regret-that-he-didn-t-get-more.html.

109. Anthony Fisher, "No, Ralph Nader Did Not Hand the 2000 Presidential Election to George W. Bush," *Reason*, August 3, 2016, https://reason.com/2016/08/03/ralph-nader-did-not-hand-2000-election/.

110. Christopher S. P. Magee, "Third-Party Candidates and the 2000 Presidential Election," *Social Science Quarterly* 84, no. 3 (September 2003), https://www.jstor.org/stable/42955889?seq=1#page_scan_tab_contents.

112. "The Great American Restoration," P2004, accessed December 16, 2019, http://p2004.org/dean/dean062303/dean062303spt.html.

115. Joel Roberts, "Dean's Scream: Not What It Seemed," CBS News, January 26 2004, https://www.cbsnews.com/news/deans-scream-not-what-it-seemed/.

120. Rob Christensen, "Echoes of John Edwards Heard in '16 Presidential Campaign," Impact 2020, February 17, 2016, https://www.mcclatchydc.com/news/politics-government/election/article60844022.html.

120. Peter Hart, "Taking Offense at Edwards," FAIR, February 1, 2008, https://fair.org/extra/taking-offense-at-edwards. "The 'three Hs,' as they would become known in the mainstream press."

127. Michael Nelson, "Barack Obama: Campaigns and Elections," UVA Miller Center, accessed December 16, 2019, https://millercenter.org/president/obama/campaigns-and-elections.

128. "Transcript: MSNBC and Telemundo's Clinton–Sanders Town Hall," NBC News, February 18, 2016, https://www.nbcnews.com/politics/2016-election/transcript-msnbc-telemundo-clinton-sanders-town-hall-n520781.

131. Greg Price, "Hillary Clinton Robbed Bernie Sanders of the Democratic Nomination, According to Donna Brazile," *Newsweek*, November 2, 2017, https://www.newsweek.com/clinton-robbed-sanders-dnc-brazile-699421.

135. Maxim Lott, "Americans Warming to Socialism Over Capitalism, Polls Show," Fox News, January 4, 2019, https://www.foxnews.com/politics/americans-warming-to-socialism-over-capitalism-polls-show.

146. Ted Rall, "Bernie Sanders Needs to Move Left," *Wall Street Journal*, February 25, 2019, https://www.wsj.com/articles/bernie-sanders-needs-to-move-left-11551137743.

171. Foreign countries booked blocks of rooms at Trump hotels that they had no intention of using.

ALSO BY TED RALL

"A dramatic, evocative, thoughtful and very accessible account of one of the most important stories of the century—and one of the most ominous, unless citizens are roused to action to rein in abusive state power." —Noam Chomsky

$16.95 • ISBN: 978-1-60980-635-4

Donald Trump, who never held political office, pulled off his ultimate acquisition: the hostile takeover of the Republican Party. Everyone was shocked—except those who knew him.

$16.95 • ISBN: 978-1-60980-758-0

"[T]his swift-paced and thought-provoking book is ultimately hopeful about whether this pope has 'Made the Church Great Again,' providing readers a jumping-off point to keep questioning." —*Publishers Weekly*

$17.95 • ISBN: 978-1-60980-760-3

UPDATED 2020 EDITION
"More than a campaign biography, this graphic narrative traces the decline and possible resurgence of liberalism within the Democratic Party . . . An effective primer on a strong voice from the left to counter the Democrats' rightward shift."
—*Kirkus Reviews*

$17.95 • ISBN: 978-1-64421-032-1